TAKE YOUR PILLS
AND GO TO
YOUR ROOM

TAKE YOUR PILLS AND GO TO YOUR ROOM

A MOM'S TRUE STORY ABOUT LIFE, CHILDREN, AND ADHD

JANICE JONES

Outskirts Press, Inc.
Denver, Colorado

Bible references from the KJV Bible.

Outskirts Press, Inc.
http://www.outskirtspress.com

ISBN: 978-1-4327-7733-3

Outskirts Press and the "OP" logo are trademarks belonging to Outskirts Press, Inc.

PRINTED IN THE UNITED STATES OF AMERICA

To all the children

Contents

Acknowledgments

(Psalm 127:3–5)

THANK YOU, MY Lord and Savior, Jesus Christ, for first and foremost loving us with perfect love.

God's example of love and parenting is a blessing that is available to us all. It's easy to understand and to apply when we come to know the Lord and experience His loving parenting personally.

Jesus forgives tirelessly and allows repetition patiently. He parents us with guidance and solid boundaries. He intervenes when necessary, yet allows consequences for infractions when appropriate. Our Heavenly Father does all of this in order that we might have the most important asset of life: FREEDOM OF CHOICE. This book would not be possible without Him, His creation, His wisdom, and His love.

Thank you, my son, Wesley, for the experience of a lifetime. What a blessing from God you are!

Thank you, my daughter, Jami, for not only inspiring the title for the book, but also the idea to write it. What a treasure from God you are!

To all my children I extend my heartfelt thanks. Both the children that grew in my womb and the children that grew in my home. They all have grown in my heart and filled it with love. I love these children, and my life would not be the same without them. They have kept my spirit young and my life full. Thank you, Chris, Sarah, Cynthia, Katie, Daelin, Colin, Melissa, Kayla, Keith, Kylie, Josh, James, Brian, Tyron, Marissa, Jacob, and Tyson, for filling my home with joy.

I cannot say enough about the importance of the support of my friends and family who encouraged me for years to write and finish this book. Thank you, Kevin, Penny, Cindy, Val, Renee, Linda, my brothers Bill and Chris, and a special thanks to Jim.

Take Your Pills And Go To Your Room is here! Yes!

Foreword

HOW DO I begin to capture on paper all God has taught me as I experienced raising a child who has ADHD? (The cursor on the computer screen sits flashing.) There is so much to share. It's overwhelming, and rightly so. The child with ADHD is guaranteed to be overwhelming. Research and diagnosis as well as medication and parenting can leave one feeling exhausted and numb. Research alone is all-encompassing. From doctors' waiting room pamphlets and magazine articles, to Internet information and books, many parents of children with ADHD find themselves inundated with information and overwhelmed with decisions. Medicating and schooling are additional challenges, and everyday management finds parents ending the day without the energy to brush their teeth. But there is HOPE and BEAUTY in every day. There is PROGRESS and VICTORY in every hour. And there is an abundance of LAUGHTER and LOVE in every moment.

I did not write this book to tell what I have researched and what I have read. I wrote to share what I have experienced and what I know. The information in each chapter is not scientific. It is real life. This book is simply my true story.

I often describe ADHD as "life times ten." Of this much I am certain: I am ten times blessed! I am ten times loved! I am ten times alive!

As I journeyed through the years of my son's upbringing, I often said, "Life is an adventure! And I am going to give it everything I have. What I have is what God gives to me."

God richly blessed me with a child who has ADHD.

Section I
The Basics

1

Diagnosis

"OK. We have a problem."
(Matthew 18:1–6)

I REMEMBER THE day that I first heard my son may have ADHD.

I was sitting in the pediatric exam room at my family physician's facility with my seven-year-old son Wesley. We were there for a routine school physical before he would begin second grade. Wes was doing what he did best . . . MOVING. He was filling the "boring" waiting time with something to do. He was climbing and jumping and crawling and rolling and touching anything he could reach. He weighed himself, measured himself, tried to listen to his own heart, and take his own blood pressure.

I sat in a chair and without looking up from the magazine I was attempting to read said,

"Sit down, baby."

"Get up, honey."

"Get down."

"Stand up."

"No jumping."

"OK, that's enough."

"Put it away, NOW."

"No more, Wes."

"OK, get in the chair."

"Sit still!"

These short commands had become my primary vocabulary. When Dr. Williams entered the room, he performed his exam on Wesley, and then sat in the chair opposite me at the desk.

As he wrote in Wes's chart he asked, "How has Wesley been doing in school?"

"Well, he's doing all right, I guess. But his teachers have told me that he has trouble sitting still and disrupts the class. They say it takes him longer to do his work. I know he is very active and strong-willed."

Dr. Williams was quiet for a moment. Then he said, "I think he may have ADHD. We could try some medication and see if it helps."

I recall my reaction well.

I had heard of ADHD and was convinced it was highly overrated and overdiagnosed and that too many children were on medication just because they were active and strong-willed. Having my child medicated in order to control him would be OVER MY DEAD BODY. After hearing the reasons for my opposition, Dr. Williams attempted to explain how the medication might help Wesley. But I was extremely skeptical and would hear no more of it.

My son's behavior was my normalcy. He was my only child at the time. I knew no different. This was the fruit of my womb that pushed and rolled and kicked inside of me for, I'm sure, all nine months. This was my beautiful, dark curly-haired, bright hazel-eyed ball of energy that toddled about my home and brought laughter and happiness to all who knew him. This was my preschool pirate—policeman—pogo-pouncing—paper-plane-flying—Popsicle-sucking—popcorn-eating—passionate little person. This was my schoolboy bicycle buddy who woke up excited about what he did yesterday and what he would do today. This was my life!

In the weeks that followed, I did much reflecting and some wondering. Wesley's biological father and I had been separated and divorced since our son was two years of age. The two years that followed were full of change and adjustment. My mother did not work and was Wesley's care provider while I worked and schooled. Soon, I met a wonderful man who took both of us into his life and married him. This joining was good but not without challenges.

One night, early in our marriage, Wes's behavioral issues became alarmingly obvious.

My husband, who had never been married and had no children, took on the family responsibilities with great motivation and a willingness to understand. However, he had some expectations that were important to him. Sleeping ALONE with his wife was one of them. Since the divorce, Wesley and I had been sleeping together. It gave us both a sense of security and bonding after being away from each other all day and no longer living in our own home. The evening routine of reading, singing, and falling asleep was nurturing for both of us. My husband was supportive of the reading and singing routine. He, however, was not receptive to my remaining in Wesley's bed with him until he went to sleep. He felt that the reason Wes came into our room during the night was because of my sending him off to sleep lying beside him. I was interested in supporting my husband. He was wonderful to both of us, and this was important to him.

What we did this particular evening, however, proved only to set us up for disaster.

Kevin had come home from work earlier than expected Wesley was asleep with me in bed. (This was a compromise I incorporated for nights when Kevin was at work.) My husband, of course, wanted Wes out of our bed and in his own. As one can imagine, upon awakening when being carried to his room, four-year-old Wesley was terribly unhappy. He tried to follow us out of his room and refused to remain in his bed. It soon became a power struggle, a test of the wills that we felt we must win. The gentle approach lasted only minutes. We tried the assertive, persistent approach next. We firmly told the child NO and held the door shut. Wesley cried and yelled and screamed at the top of his lungs. This went on for a long time. Our wills were just as strong, but our bodies were terribly tired. Kevin then devised a way to tie the door shut. He and I sat on the couch for hours while Wes's cries echoed down the hallway. He fluctuated from quieter pleas for release to extreme anger and physical assaults on the door.

It was while sitting on the couch this late evening, three hours into my sleep time, that I looked at my new husband and said, "I will NEVER do this again. THIS has got to be the WRONG way."

I believe that what resulted from the evening's events was Wesley's sudden awareness that he was at war with his new father. In his mind, he was fighting for what was first and rightfully his—his mother. This was a new concept. For years, we dealt with this problem of our own creation.

The evening ended in a compromise. A plan was made that all three of us could live with. Wesley's nighttime routine of reading and singing remained unchanged. I would leave the room before he fell asleep. However, if he woke in the night, he was allowed to come into our room where a sleeping mat on the floor by my side of the bed was pre-made for him. He was not to wake us, but to lie down in the bedding and go to sleep.

It is my belief that none of this should have been necessary. The one sure thing about children is that they grow and change. I believe Wesley would have outgrown his need to fall asleep with his mother in his own good time. Instead, he insisted on sleeping with me any chance he got, up to the age of twelve. At this age, Wes decided he was too old to sleep with his mother. I believe he would have come to this realization much sooner in life had we not made it the issue it became.

Recalling the "tying the door shut" story has always embarrassed me. Because it has done this, it has also stayed with me. And it was with me the day Dr. Williams made his suggestion.

In the fall of Wesley's second-grade year, Kevin's parents made a visit. During this visit I told my mother-in-law, Erika, of my recent upsetting doctor's visit. She then told me about her experience with my husband when he was young and how it led her to find what was called the Feingold Diet. Erika endorsed Dr. Feingold's theory that many food additives and other things found naturally in what we eat are responsible for some children's behavioral problems. I was intrigued by the idea. After all, I had been a Seventh-Day Adventist all my life. The idea that what we eat greatly affects our mind and body had been implanted in me at a young age.

After Kevin's parents returned home, I sought out Dr. Feingold's information. At my local bookstore I found his book, *Why Your Child Is Hyperactive,* and read it cover to cover. In this book, I read numerous case studies Feingold had conducted that caused him to create the diet. It became his experience that he was able to assist families of children with severe behavior problems when they followed the diet carefully. In many of his participating patients, he was able to greatly reduce their need for medications, and in some, was able to get them off medication completely. I liked this idea. Upon completing the book, I decided to give the diet a try. My husband, in spite of his vivid negative memories of deprivation while on the diet, agreed. Wesley was informed of what I wanted to do and why and also agreed to participate.

Dr. Feingold believed that all artificial colors and flavors, and artificial sweeteners and preservatives, were responsible for behavioral problems in children and adults with ADHD. He gave caffeine questionable credit as well. He recommended complete abstinence from foods containing these substances. I, being independent of thought and strong-willed myself, slightly altered the diet. I was happy to have my son abstain from artificial food additives and caffeine. However, I was not willing to completely abstain from foods containing natual components that the diet listed as possible causes to behavioral problems. According to Dr. Feingold, these substances were found in many furits and vegetables. Wesley loved fruits and vegetables. I refused to remove these from his diet.

For one week we conducted our own experiment. The entire family followed my version of the diet. Wesley knew that at the end of seven days he would be able to indulge in a moderate amount of food he had had to abstain from.

During the week we began to notice subtle changes. Wes seemed to be more even tempered and had not acted out to any real degree. However, what happened at the end of the week was downright scary!

On day seven, Wesley was allowed to have a handful of Gummy Worm candy and three maraschino cherries. Within thirty minutes, he had had a terrible argument with two of his closest friends. He was so angry and agitated that he cried continuously for forty-five minutes. He screamed out how he hated his friends and how he never wanted them to swim or fish in his pond, ride his horses, or play in his tree house, or even see him again. Needless to say, our little test was conclusive. It became very obvious to all three of us that Dr. Feingold had something.

I encourage anyone to research Dr. Feingold's information and decide if the diet is right for their child or family members or themselves. It is obviously a harmless diet that can only better one's health.

Yet, the diet was not without problems.

Firstly, it will always be true that with anything you choose to make an issue of concerning the well-being of your child, there can and probably will be parental discrepancies and inconsistencies.

My husband was (as he lovingly called himself) "detail oriented."

This type of personality cares deeply and is very particular about many things in life. They do things by the book. They tend to see mostly black and white. Therefore, their expectations and dealings with issues can seem intense and even inappropriate to other, more relaxed personalities.

My approach to the diet for Wesley and Kevin's approach were as different as night and day. Kevin believed that once you start the diet you are not allowed off it. No breaks permitted. He had trouble with the idea that if Wesley was on the diet, it would be better if his parents were not seen eating forbidden food. I, on the other hand, believed that in order to avoid overwhelming feelings of deprivation resulting in open rebellion, Wes should be allowed moderate amounts of forbidden food on special occasions, such as birthdays and holidays. I also felt that it would be rude to tell the child, "You must have a real fruit slush that is clear in color, but I am going to have a pretty blue coconut one." After all, it was a healthier way for me to eat also.

Secondly, it is a DIET. Diets take willpower. When you're a parent who has put your child on a diet, you have to have willpower enough for two. Any of us who has tried to follow a diet knows how difficult it can be. Due to the nature of diets, one instantly feels some level of deprivation. Forbidden food becomes ten times more appealing, attractive, and delicious. It lurks in every corner of the store—friends' and neighbors' homes—at school—theaters—restaurants—and picnics and potlucks. Also, unless a parent straps a child to their side 24/7, policing and enforcing the diet at all times is impossible. Unless the child is extremely self-disciplined (which, in my opinion, makes a diagnosis of ADHD a very likely mistake) or has been brought into submission by terrible fear, he/she is guaranteed to find ways to cheat on the diet.

Due to these things, my version of the Feingold diet alone was an inadequate treatment.

By the time Wesley was nine years old, we knew we needed to understand more about ADHD. After two broken bedrooms windows—two damaged bedroom doors and doorjambs—a hole in the wall of the hallway and one in the dining room—broken toys—deteriorating grades at school and school suspensions—we knew we needed advanced intervention and assistance. This otherwise beautiful—intelligent—happy—energetic—pleasant child desperately needed his parents to seek out and find adequate and appropriate help. God was speaking.

Kevin and I sought help for Wesley by first having him evaluated by a child psychologist. Erika had researched and found one to her liking in the nearby city where she lived.

We arrived on a Friday evening at the office of Dr. Perlmutter, a child psychologist who came highly recommended to us. Her office was large with a full-size couch, large, cushy pillows, and surrounding comfortable chairs.

Kevin and I spoke with her about our son, and she also talked with Wes.

I do not recall what Wesley was doing during our first meeting. I'm sure I was successfully ignoring continuous movement. I do not recall that Wes said anything terribly revealing concerning his suspected disorder. But I will never forget what Dr. Perlmutter said at the close of our initial meeting.

This very seasoned psychologist looked at me and said, "I can tell you without evaluation that Wesley has ADHD. He's got it in spades. It's probably one of the worst cases I have ever seen."

My first reaction was that I knew she had to be wrong about "the worst case she had ever seen." However, it was on this evening that I began to embrace the idea that Wes may truly have ADHD.

Dr. Perlmutter's evaluation of Wesley took one full day and half of the next. She spent most of her weekend assessing my son through various tests. Although Wes would rather have been doing something else, he seemed to like Dr. Perlmutter and enjoyed the activities she used to test him. When she was finished, we all met once again in her office where she reported that her testing supported her initial suspicions. She highlighted some of her testing techniques and Wes's responses to them. Dr. Perlmutter advised us that these tests, combined with her experience and time spent with Wesley, concluded a diagnosis of ADHD and Impulsivity Disorder (a commonly associated condition). She told us she would have a full written report for us as soon as possible and suggested that we begin stimulant medication therapy immediately and enroll ourselves in parenting classes for parents of children with ADHD.

That afternoon, my husband and I decided to take Dr. Perlmutter's advice. Little did we know that we were about to embark on a whole new way of thinking and acting.

The following are my top four MOST IMPORTANT THINGS GOD HAS TAUGHT ME about raising my child with ADHD. I believe these to be absolutely crucial and that the parent who uses these tips is at an advantage. So much so, that they are listed now in the first chapter.

Choose Your Battles

DAVID COMES TO my mind frequently as I relate to his human nature and aspire to walk with God as he did. Likewise, I think of David and the battle with Goliath when I think of choosing your battles.

While still a minor and barely anointed, young David must have already understood this concept as God had shown him. When he bent down to pick up the stone he would use to overcome the Philistines' giant challenger, Goliath, he picked up four additional stones as well. Some theologians teach that he did this perposely and symbolically and not due to any doubt, fear or thought of missing his mark. David had sound faith in the Lord and in the physical ability God had given him. He had become skilled with the sling and sword as a shepherd, overcoming large predators many times while protecting his father's flocks. On the battlefield that day, David knew that he must not only conquer Goliath, but eventually the four additional giants known in the land or Israel would never have victory over its enemies. He paid no attention to the army of smaller soldiers that day or worried about the armies of smaller soldiers to come (1 Samuel 17).

Jesus addressed our nature to sweat the small stuff when responding to Martha's frustration over Mary not helping her to properly entertain guests. He called to Martha's attention her needless worry of little matters and the importance of choosing what really matters (Luke 10:38–42).

Some issues are important and must be addressed. But remember that in many cases, what you decide not to make an issue of becomes powerless to become a problem.

I once explained the concept of Choosing Your Battles with the following analogy:

Imagine a water trough and faucet flowing water and particles of various sizes continually into the trough. The trough is our capacity for dealing with life's problems. The flowing water is life. The particles are problems or issues. The larger particles sink to the bottom while the smaller particles float to the top and spill over the tank. Hang on to the big things and deal with them. But let the little things float to the top and spill over the tank. Let them go!

As is well-known, child rearing takes a lot of energy. The child with ADHD can be an energy sapper. Save your energy for truly important issues. You will need it!

Offer Choices

IN GOD'S INFINITE wisdom, He gave mankind the privilege to choose (Genesis 2:15–17; Joshua 24:15; Isaiah 7:15).

When anyone is offered choices, life just looks a little brighter. Creative parents are capable of maintaining better order in the home by simply creating choices that result in the desired outcome. When one is able to incorporate choices in rules, the perception becomes less a "rule" and, thus, more difficult to break. It loses rebellion appeal!

One of Wesley's rules when very young was that he must wear his nicer clothes for school and other outings and play clothes for everyday play. However, what he wore on a given day from these two categories of clothing was ENTIRELY up to him. Matching color or accessories was not an issue and "making a statement" was allowed. Occasionally, we would make suggestions. But the final choice was his alone. Whatever he came up with was regarded as "perfect"—"handsome"—"very nice." We spent a few years taking Wes places sporting cowboy boots with shorts, belts worn on clothes with no belt loops, his latest Halloween costume, or favorite pajamas. It made us smile and allowed him to express his independence in a harmless and positive way. Of course, during his teen years, this freedom of expression that was once considered adorable became embarrassing. But it didn't matter. The principle was the same, and the end result was a young man who chose to take pride in his appearance.

Even simple choices throughout the day can have a positive effect on attitude. Everyday choices like what to eat for breakfast—where to sit in the car—choosing products at the market—which dessert to make for after dinner—which nighttime toy to sleep with—or which book to read before bed can help a child to feel he/she is an important member of the family, has responsibility, and is in control of their lives.

In Wes's teen years, choices where reality could be used as leverage became very useful.

We supplied Wesley his first vehicle. But it was his responsibility to fuel and help insure it. Whether he found work and made money was entirely up to him. We knew how importance independence and transportation was to our son, and the strategy worked very well. And, continuing to include Wes on smaller, everyday decisions during his teens also improved attitude.

In both Wesley's young and teen years, the sting of being asked to obey when he didn't want to could be lessened by a quick reminder of his freedom of choice and brief description of each choice's consequence or outcome. I would end with, "It's up to you. You decide." More times than not, Wes made the right choice. Yet, if he didn't, I had to be prepared to follow through with the consequences.

Incorporating choices into rules and obedience expectations can be very useful when managing ADHD.

Pray

THERE IS NO better reason to pray than for the well-being of a child. Yet my independent nature made giving anything to God difficult for me.

But the Lord in His great wisdom cleverly spoke to me through avenues I was most sensitive to. Only on hindsight did I realize that it was God who moved me so strongly toward certain ideas and in certain directions.

I know that God led me every step of the way, in spite of myself. Communication with God is POWERFUL (Mark 11:24–25; Romans 8:26–27; 1 Thessalonians 5:16–18).

Further studies on prayer are abundantly available for anyone who would like to learn more about this open channel of communication with God. But be careful. Do not allow yourself to be overwhelmed. Some opinions can lead one to feel their prayers cannot be heard unless they are meeting specific requirements. Many times this is not the desire of the author or person sharing his/her opinion, but an inadvertent misguiding. Communion with the Lord is crazily simple as He hears our every thought and speaks to us continually. We just have to recognize His voice.

No matter where you are or what you are doing, picture Jesus with you, because He is (Emanuel—God with us). Focus on Him and start talking. Be sure to ask Him a question, then tune into the spontaneous flow of thoughts that come to you. If they are comforting (Comforter), edifying (Counselor), and bring you peace (Prince of Peace), then you have just heard from the Lord! Much of the time, this experience will also make your heart leap with joy.

Conversely, our thoughts are apt to be influenced by evil when not focused on God. These influences are just as easy to identify. One will not feel comforted but torn (destroyer, adversary) and overcome with a general sense of hopelessness or low self-worth (accuser, Beelzebub—father of lies) and feel as though their heart is heavy and depressed. I encourage the study called *Communion with God* by Mark Virkler, where I learned the above tips on recognizing God's voice (Matthew 1:23; John 14:16–18; Isaiah 9:6; 1 Peter 5:8; Revelation 12:9–10; John 8:42–44).

Pray without ceasing.

Forgive and Forget

THE PARABLE (STORY) told by Jesus of the lost son is one of the most beautiful explanations of forgiveness in the Bible. The father not only forgives his son his poor judgment, he celebrates the child's good judgment. The father does not speak of anything regarding experienced consequences of his son's negative behavior but instead, he forgets it and focuses on the reward of his positive behavior. The story is a wonderful example of how God parents us. He forgives, forgets, and celebrates! (Luke 15:11–32)

Jesus' ministry of healing the human body was not ever without the even more important healing of the human soul. He mended man's broken and dying soul by simply forgiving him. And no soul was too shameful to forgive. From the woman caught in the very act of adultery to the thief on the cross, Jesus showed us that forgiveness has no limits, including forgiving those who are not asking to be forgiven and who seem unforgivable (John 8:1–11; Luke 23:32–43).

Where would ANY of us be without the amazing blessing of forgiveness? No matter our spiritual convictions or beliefs, all of humankind understands this concept. We have either been blessed by forgiveness or suffered due to the lack of it. If you're a parent who struggles with the act of forgiveness, it is possible that you did not feel well forgiven as a child. And/or you have trouble forgiving yourself for your own imperfections. Guilt and low self-esteem are by-products of unforgiveness. These can cause anger and depression. Adults and children who believe they are not forgivable feel they are unlovable. The result is a life less fulfilling with potential for significant dysfunction.

If you think you may be this kind of parent, BREAK THE CYCLE! Do it now! Help yourself so you can help your child. Seek professional help if needed.

When we realize that God is perfect and we are not and that He forgives us perfectly, only then can we begin to understand the concept of "forgetting."

I had a pastor explain God's forgiveness to me in a way I've not since forgotten.

I was struggling with guilt, anger, and depression due to the burden of unforgiveness. I couldn't forgive MYSELF. My pastor took a piece of paper and a pencil. Near the bottom center of the page he drew a tree. At the top left corner of the page he drew the sun. From the tree, to the right lower corner of the paper he drew the tree's shadow/shade.

My pastor explained, "The sun is GOD'S LOVE. The tree is SIN. The shadow is GUILT." Then he turned the pencil over and erased the tree but left the shadow and said, "Jesus forgives the sin—cuts down the tree. Why is there still a shadow where only the Son's love should remain?"

There should be no shadows remaining in anyone's life, and especially in the lives of our children as they grow and learn. Yes, I believe it is ten times important for the child with ADHD. Gift your child with the blessing of a clean slate as Jesus does for you.

It is my understanding that children tend to view God the way they view their parents. I believe this to be true.

WOW! What a responsibility!

It should not be taken lightly. But, do not let this responsibility overwhelm you. The difference between us and God is evident. We are not perfect. God is. Love you child with this in mind, and he/she will love himself/herself. It is imperative to your child's psychological well-being.

As time progressed, I, too, progressed from my state of ignorance that day in Dr. William's office. I came to know that ADHD is a scientific and medically legitimate, physiological disorder. I began to understand that in order to obtain an accurate diagnosis, one must complete both a psychological and physical evaluation performed by appropriate professionals. I became convinced that I must educate myself continually on all aspects of ADHD, and then follow my instincts. I knew my "gut" was God talking to me and that when God spoke, I should listen.

As my husband and I traveled home after Wesley's evaluation and diagnosis, God was speaking loud and clear. It was time to take the next step.

2

Medication

"OK, we need medication."
(EZEKIEL 47:12)

IT WAS A typical day at home with the children.

Wesley was twelve years old and his little sister, Jami, was two. Summer vacation was in full swing and as was typical any time of year, the house was bustling with cousins and the neighborhood children, anxious to begin the summer activities planned for the day. Wes was also in his typical morning state of mind. He had been out of bed for less than an hour and needed breakfast and his medication. Mornings often found him fussy, intolerant, and unable to control his impulsivity. For Wesley, this was his MOUTH.

I stood at the changing table in Jami's room, getting her dressed for the day. Jami's indecipherable chatter had recently changed to English, and she was busy jabbering about this and that. The other children were restlessly waiting in the living room, playfully tormenting each other as children do. After being asked to perform a morning duty, Wes snapped back with a disrespectful remark and adamant refusal. He was verbally reprimanded and asked again to perform the task. Wesley retorted again with an even more defiant statement. He was then warned of the consequences I would inflict upon him if he didn't "snap out of it," and the requested duty became a command.

The volume of Wes's argumentative words increased. At this point, I met his volume with more decibels and yelled from the baby's room into the kitchen.

"Wesley, take your pills and go to your room!"

Jami, who had been listening quietly for a few moments, then said, "Yeah ess! Take pills 'n go room!"

Instantly the house was filled with laughter. I couldn't help but laugh out loud along with the other children. Even Wesley's mood had quickly changed, and he chuckled under his breath. And the baby laughed because she had made a funny.

It is always good to find humor in life. Still, the echo of my words to Wes coming from my toddler got my attention that day. I realized three things:

How often I said them.

How I sounded when I said them.

And the title of the book I would one day write.

When Mrs. Perlmutter diagnosed Wesley, she advised us to use Ritalin, one of the first and most commonly used medications for the treatment of ADHD at that time. She also recommended a high dose and frequent administration of the medication for his daily regimen. Mrs. Perlmutter strongly encouraged us to get name brand Ritalin and also not to use any slow-release versions of the medication. She insisted that the generic brands had poor quality control and that the slow-release Ritalin would not be strong enough for Wes. Mrs. Perlmutter recommended a total of 32½ milligrams of Ritalin per day, administered as follows:

Morning – 10 mgs
Noon – 10 mgs
Afternoon – 7.5 mgs
Evening – 5 mgs

We took a copy of her recommendation to our personal physician who wrote the prescription, no questions asked.

I never dreamed I would medicate my child for behavioral management. Nevertheless, there I was handing my beautiful, physically healthy son a little white pill. Again, due to my being independent of thought and strong-willed in nature, I tried the generic Ritalin and Adderall, a milder mixture of several stimulants that last longer in the system. It became quickly obvious that Mrs. Perlmutter was right. The generic, regular Ritalin did not work as well or last as long. And the Adderall also had little effect.

The effects of Ritalin were almost instantaneous. Throughout the first week of school, Wesley's teacher reported noticeable behavioral improvements. She said that he seemed able to sit still longer, was less distractible, and was able to better stay on task. His outbursts were less frequent, and if he did become upset, the episode was less intense.

We, too, noticed behavioral changes at home. Wes was more receptive and willing when asked to do boring, uninteresting, and repetitive tasks in the home. He seemed less short fused with his friends and family. Wesley's life and ours became less negative and less stressful.

What an amazing thing, this medication! WHAT? What an amazing thing this MEDICATION? The positive results were undeniable. Yet, God was speaking, "This is good, but there's more."

The following is what God has taught me about medication and medicating:

Be Informed

IF YOU DECIDE that medication is necessary, become well informed about the medications available. Learn why each one works, how it works, and what side effects it may have. Don't let side effects stop you from giving the medication a try. All medication manufactures are required to list any possible side effects, no matter how rare. When I decided to medicate my child, the primary deciding factor was that I was just going to try it. If I didn't like what it did, it was simple. I would discontinue it.

Pharmaceutical information is available through many avenues. Talk to your doctor or pharmacist or research the medications yourself. I found it interesting to know if the medication was made from natural products or synthetic and what class it belonged to. But more important, it was helpful for me to understand the mechanism of action of each drug. This explains how the medication works in the body.

Wesley suffered two side effects from Ritalin.

As is true with most stimulants, they can have withdrawal signs and symptoms (such as irritability) and cause significant appetite suppression. Eventually I learned that natural stimulants (such as caffeine) worked well when dealing with the nuisance of withdrawal. It could also be used as a substitute when a longer-acting dose of stimulant was not necessary or unavailable. The side effect of appetite suppression was much more alarming for me. I was about to discontinue the medication due to Wes's weight loss. He had lost seven pounds off of his already-slender body before I realized what we needed to do.

Most oral medications take approximately thirty minutes for the digestive system to absorb it and release it into the bloodstream.

The Ritalin Wes was taking lasted exactly three hours (to the minute). It was simple. Medicate him at mealtime, as he sat down to eat. Thirty minutes was plenty of time for him to finish a meal and three hours was not too long to wait for another. It worked beautifully! His weight came back up, and I was happy again.

Once again, use the resources available to you. Find out all you can about any medication available for the treatment of ADHD. Then talk to your doctor about trying it.

Experiment

EVERY ADHD PATIENT is unique and responds to medication differently. What works for one person might not for another. There are new medications being introduced continually as well as older medications that have stood the test of time. Try what you and your doctor feel are best and evaluate the results. If you are not satisfied, try something else.

Over time, we also tried new medications. As Wesley became older, he would initiate a change. Each time the decision was made to return to Ritalin as either Wes or my husband and I did not feel he received the same benefit.

Treat the Whole Person

BE CAREFUL NOT to become caught up in the false sense of total wellness that medication can give. There is so much more to the management of ADHD. Medication is only capable of assisting you. It is not a quick fix.

For the child or adult with ADHD, every aspect of life is multiplied significantly and distractions lurk in every corner of their world. Medication can assist with this problem. Nevertheless, it is medication. It is beneficial only when used properly, according to individual needs and with compliance. "Properly" and "according to individual needs" are person dependent. We quickly learned that Wesley benefited most from the 10 milligram dose of Ritalin in the morning and at noon, especially when in school. The afternoon and evening doses were not as crucial. It became our routine to medicate Wes (and later have him medicate himself) at breakfast and lunch. We understood that medicating before bed was not recommended and did not do this. By the time Wesley was a senior in high school, he found he was able to discontinue regular scheduled doses, substitute caffeine, and medicate himself only as needed.

Even after embracing the idea of medication, I refused to become dependent upon it in order to manage my son. I refused to allow my son or others of my family to depend upon it or focus on it. It was merely a tool to assist us, nothing more.

I knew that I wanted Wes to learn to manage himself, to understand his disorder and his medication. In order to do so, I had to understand his disorder and medication.

Educate Yourself

INFORMATION ABOUT ADHD can be easily found in bookstores, libraries, or on the Internet. I also STRONGLY recommend attending seminars that include ADHD topics and speakers or viewing audio or video recordings of the same.

My fortune was very good the day my mother-in-law discovered seminars close to me put on by the Learning Disabilities Association of America (LDA). These seminars were geared for schoolteachers and parents. They were FANTASTIC! I was greatly helped as I listened to many well-versed speakers, including medical doctors, doctors of child psychology, and experienced teachers and authors. The seminars also hosted a selection of booths where one could purchase books, audio, and video materials, as well as educational toys and computer programs for children. The cost to attend was very reasonable and the benefit was priceless.

If you are skeptical about having your child evaluated and medicated, but are curious about the possibilities of him/her having ADHD, take advantage of the various resources of information available and submerge yourself in them. Search online to learn more about the LDA of America.

The decision to medicate my son did not come easy. It came with pain and sweat and prayer. I will never regret making this difficult decision. Medicating Wesley was the right thing to do.

3

Schooling

"OK . . . We are going to finish school!"
(Proverbs 22:6)

THE BIBLE TELLS us that King Solomon was gifted by God with superior wisdom and is known to be the author of most of the book of Proverbs. The proverb above has brought comfort and encouragement to many parents and childcare providers through the ages.

Anyone who has a passion to teach children can become discouraged when they do not see immediate results of their efforts. But God promises that if we do our best to "teach a child in the way that he should go," our efforts will eventually pay off. The passage says, "When he is OLD he will not depart from it." The Lord is telling us to do our best to teach them right, then to let them go and be patient.

Interestingly enough, as we read Solomon's amazing words of wisdom, we discover that he simply was blessed with superior common sense! God demonstrated through Solomon that true intelligence has little to do with having a head full of knowledge and more to do with having a heart full of life.

Each one of my son's teachers deserve an all-expense paid cruise, a new car, a new wardrobe, and a spot on *The Today Show* for the school year they endured. They each had something wonderful to contribute to my son's school experience. Yet, the percentage of them that were not well informed about Wes's disorder was hard for me to understand.

I specifically remember one of my son's teachers while in middle school. She was a wonderful, dedicated, and caring woman who was suffering the "Wesley Struggle." She was Wes's science teacher while in seventh grade. I lovingly dubbed her, Mrs. Spider, for reasons that will soon be evident.

Wesley had brought home several notes from his science teacher, advising whatever recent problem she had had with him and what she had done to address it. I had also spoken with her on the phone but had not yet met her.

It was Parent-Teacher Conference time, and I was spending my morning meeting each of Wes's teachers. As I walked the long hallway toward the science teacher's room, I thought about the teachers I had already met. I was pleased with Wesley's math teacher. He was a big, young, and energetic man who seemed to appreciate and understand my son's matching energy, spunk, and wit. This teacher also understood Wes's need to have limited distractions and to be allowed more time to complete assignments. I was worried, however, after meeting Wesley's computer teacher. This no-nonsense teacher had fixed expectations and reported Wes's failing grade frankly. My concern was not as much for my son as it was for her. It was my opinion that she, and people like her, were likely to live a life of repeated disappointments and frustrations.

When I arrived at Wes's science teacher's room, I found the door open and no teacher or other parents present. As I walked inside, my eyes widened and my jaw dropped. The room was COVERED in spider paraphernalia. Not a spot of paint was visible on the walls that were papered with colorful spider posters, pictures, and gadgets. Even the chalkboard was hard to locate. Several aquariums housing different spider species were scattered about the edges of the room. Hanging from the ceiling was a giant, black plastic spider, its eight legs tacked to the corners and edges and draping across the ceiling. I slowly found my way to a chair positioned at her desk and sat down. When the science teacher walked in, she introduced herself and shook my hand. Eye contact was quickly broken, however. Pinned to her left lapel was a beautiful gold spider web with green jewels sparkling at each point of the web. And, of course, sitting in the middle was a large, gold and green-jeweled SPIDER.

As had become my custom, I allowed the teacher to initiate the meeting conversation. I listened to her carefully. Her chief complaint was that Wesley would not follow instructions or commands.

When she was finished with her report, I looked at this wonderful science teacher and said, "This is an amazing room. It's beautiful. Love your pin." Then I went on. "I think I know what is causing the majority of your problems with Wes." I looked about her room again. "He's distracted. He's distracted beyond our comprehension. It is a wonder he hasn't just . . . spontaneously combusted." I turned back to the teacher. "Please, whatever you do don't change your room. But I have some ideas that might help you and Wesley."

She nodded and said with sincerity, "Please share them with me."

"My son has ADHD, as you may already know. When giving instructions to the class or addressing Wesley specifically, be certain to get and maintain eye contact with him. Without eye contact, he is not likely to process the information. He may appear to have heard you and may even acknowledge you, but later when you're frustrated because he didn't do as he was told, he will be oblivious as to why he is in trouble and respond defensively. Then the vicious cycle begins. Trust me, I know," I said with a nod and a laugh.

"Maybe I could also have Wes build a partition on his desk to use while doing his work."

"Yes," I said with a smile. "That sounds really good."

Not long after this conference, a disgusted Wesley complained, "Mom, would you stop telling my teachers stuff about 'eye contact'! One of them always says, 'Wesley . . . Wesley . . . Look into my eyes.'"

Of course, teachers who specialize in behavior disorders in children and how to educate them are very good at what they do.

However, getting Wes into the system so he could have access to these teachers was not easy.

While Wesley was in fourth grade, we made the difficult decision to pull him out of the private Christian school he had been attending since kindergarten. Again, we found ourselves subjecting him to evaluations and testing.

The Resource Division of the public school district in our area had certain criteria that a student had to meet in order to qualify for extra help. According to their test results, Wes was just shy of qualifying. We knew nothing of the specifics of academic assistance in the school setting. But we were convinced that the time to intervene on our son's behalf had come. In fact, we feared we were already behind. With persistence, we were able to persuade the resource evaluators to find a way to allow Wesley into their system. Due to his medical diagnosis of ADHD, they were able to "fudge" the scores enough to list Wes as Other Learning Impaired, thus qualifying him. We were in! It was agreed, however, that Wes would remain in a regular classroom with a resource teacher assisting the regular classroom teacher. As a result, we were exposed to all kinds of teachers. Some teachers were exceptional. Some teachers were acceptable. Some teachers were detrimental. But all were admirable and valuable.

The following is a list of things God has taught me about schooling the child with ADHD:

Be Persistent

NO ONE KNOWS your child better than you do. If you are convinced that he/she needs extra assistance academically, then do all you can to get it. We found our local public school system to be completely capable, cooperative, and helpful with special education resources for Wesley. However, WE had to initiate it. I believe the school would have picked up on this as well, but not immediately. Wes was very good at catching the attention of teachers and faculty because of behavioral problems and not academic problems. And he indeed suffered both. I decided I would do all I could to encourage focus on Wesley's academic needs. I knew Wes would do a very good job of making his behavioral help needs obvious.

With tenacity, anything you want for your child can be accomplished. Decide what it is God would have you to do for your student, and then GO GET IT.

Communicate with Teachers

THE MORE YOU and your child's teacher talk, the more likely you will develop an effective team for your student. I am not saying that I think we parents should become nagging, pestering, and always-in-the-classroom intrusions. I am saying that parents should swallow the pride and defenses we all can have about our children and open up the "chat line" with teachers. Teachers care very much about their students. When you involve them more deeply into your child's "psyche," you lasso their hearts. ADHD kids have many endearing qualities and contagious, upbeat personalities. But their behavioral problems tend to mask these wonderful traits. Communicating with your child's teacher can help them to better understand you and your student, take more notice of positive attributes, and heighten their drive to better your child's school experience.

Share Tips

ONCE YOU AND your student's teacher have opened the lines of communication, sharing successful management techniques can be very beneficial. Sometimes what works at home for you can be applied in the classroom. And just as often, what works in the classroom for your child's teacher can be applied at home.

Stay In Charge

REMEMBER, YOU'RE THE BOSS.

Once Wesley was in the school's resource (special education) system, we found ourselves attending regular meetings to discuss his progress, needs, and any behavioral obstacles. These meetings were usually at a full-size conference table where most of the chairs were occupied. In attendance were a variety of faculty, including Wes's teacher/teachers and at least one representative from the administrative and resource departments.

Don't let the feeling of being outnumbered intimidate you. After all, you are the parent of a child with ADHD. YOU CAN TAKE ON AN ARMY! Some people may find it helpful to take another adult with them to the meetings who is a trusted advocate for their child, understands their point of view, and is a good mediator. In order to allow a meeting to be the most productive for my son, I developed the following technique:

- Pray before the meeting.
- Leave your defenses at home.
- Arrive at the meeting on time with your confidence and focus intact.
- Keep an open mind.
- Make a mental note or jot down on paper any particular topic brought to your attention that you would like to address or comment on.
- Decide what you think is appropriate for your child and what you want, then TAKE THE FLOOR.
- Make eye contact. It projects and magnifies confidence.
- Work with those present to get what you want and what you think is appropriate. These are the people you will need to carry out your wishes.
- End the meeting on a positive note. Thank the staff for their efforts and time spent on behalf of your child and for what they will be doing for him/her in the future.

Limit Homework

WHEN NECESSARY, TALK with teachers about keeping homework assignments to a minimum. For most children with ADHD, a full day of school has already pushed the limits of their ability to stay on task and remain positive. Make a routine of free time after school whenever possible. I believe this to be a vital tool in the management of your student. Wesley and our entire family benefited greatly when he was allowed to do his own thing after school, even while in high school. I declined all suggestions that I enroll Wes in an after-school academics assistance program. I knew in my gut that this would be a negative experience for all of us and, therefore, unproductive. I insisted that he would be allowed his own time during after-school hours. My sanity depended on it.

Schooling the child with ADHD is a challenge for all involved. Many days are highlighted with frustrations. Teachers become frustrated when your student has pushed them beyond their abilities and resources to handle a problem. Your child becomes frustrated and ready to quit when negative experiences with teachers and faculty seem to bombard them "for no reason at all." (They truly believe this.) You add another one into your backpack full of frustrations and the notion to home school your child begins to creep into your mind.

STOP!

Your student and his/her teachers and school faculty are going to make it, and so are you. Home schooling is certainly an option to be considered, and for some parents and children, is the best option. My child with ADHD needed more time and more repetition in order for him to obtain academic and social success. He also needed the reality of life lessons that schooling outside the home exposed him to. I believe home schooling would have only postponed these lessons further into adulthood. Plus, I needed the break from Wesley just as much as he did from me.

Wrap your arms around your student's teachers and faculty and make a team circle with your child tucked snugly in the middle. Then start planning for a SERIOUS GRADUATION CELEBRATION. You're going to have one.

Section II
Day to Day

The following chapters are listed in chronologic age groups. I encourage reading all chapters, no matter the current age you are addressing. Many of the tips can be adapted and applied to any age, and examples are included.

1

Ages 4-7

"Isn't he cute . . . Very active though . . . Oh my!"

I CAN TELL you the exact day my then new friend Kevin passed the Wesley Test.

Kevin arrived at my parents' home where Wes and I had been living since the divorce to pick me up for a date. It was late in the evening and very near Wesley's bedtime. As was common, Wes was showing no signs of winding down for the day. He jumped and tumbled around the house and bombarded Kevin with endless chants of "Watch me! Look at me! Can you do this?" Kevin graciously watched his every move and answered his every question. Then he did it.

Kevin challenged Wes to laps up and down the stairs by saying, "I bet you can't go up and down these stairs ten times."

Without hesitation Wesley responded, "Yes, I can!" and proceeded to demonstrate his precision and speed in stair lapping.

His little, agile body thumped and jumped over the stairs, and he panted with pride at the end of each lap. (These included two flights and a landing.) But the closer Wes neared the tenth lap, the slower his pace of climb and descent became. By the time he "won the bet," Wesley was happy to don his pajamas, crawl into a lap, and rock in the rocking chair. Kevin was already well on his way, but that night he became a keeper. So, when he asked me to marry him, my answer was a premeditated—yes!

It was a wonder, however, that the man did not run down the aisle and out the door on the day of our wedding.

It was April and a beautiful spring afternoon. The trees surrounding the church were full of blossoms, and the air was sweet and warm. The majestic, wooden sanctuary was made beautiful and simple with white lilies left after an Easter service. The guest list was small, making for a relaxed and comfortable atmosphere.

The ceremony began as the large pipe organ began to play. I could not see but was aware that the minister, Kevin, and his groomsmen had walked out and took their places, and that Wesley, the ring bearer, and my bridesmaids had made their way down the aisle. With my daddy's arm hooked in mine, he looked down at me. His blue eyes smiled in approval as his strong hand patted mine. We walked down the long aisle, and he gave me away. I took my place beside Kevin, and the minister began his ceremonial address. It was only a few minutes, however, before little Wesley's ability to stand still and at attention expired. The distractions of the people in the congregation (even though they were sitting very still and quiet) and the need to move had overcome him.

As I attempted to concentrate on the minister and Kevin, I could not ignore the constant tugging and pulling at my skirt as Wes used me for balance while he jumped up and down the two steps behind us. Without looking down, I grabbed his hand in an attempt to assist him in standing still. It wasn't long before I lost his hand and Wesley turned to face the guests seated in the pews. Out of the corner of my eye, it appeared he was, at least, standing still.

Then I heard my mother's voice as quietly as she could say, "Wesley . . . no," and the congregation chuckle.

I turned to see my son demonstrating to the congregation the successful technique for picking your nose. Needless to say, the atmosphere of reverence was gone. But what remained was just as lovely. Ice was broken, hearts were lightened, and smiles were prevalent.

While viewing the pictures many days later, I saw my normalcy from a different perspective. Moments captured were as follows:

- Wesley running down the aisle upon his turn in the procession . . .
- Wesley wiggling at my side during the ceremony, his shirt coming untucked on one side . . .
- Wesley facing the congregation, his shirt completely untucked on one side . . .
- Wesley refusing to stand up for a posed picture, his shirt coming untucked on the other side . . .
- Wesley leaping back down the aisle after pictures, his shirt completely untucked on both sides . . .
- Wesley at the reception . . .
- Wesley moving here . . .
- Wesley moving there . . .

With each chronologic shot, Wes became less clothed and his mouth more covered in punch stain. By the time the birdseed was thrown and we kissed him good-bye before departing for our honeymoon, Wesley had also lost his belt, new shoes, and suit jacket and was covered in reception food smudges and droppings.

Wes's Gerber Baby good looks, adorable charm, and activity level always caught attention. Even though he was exhausting to watch and keep up with, his entertaining antics, agile coordination, and natural wit made it hard to take one's eyes off him. However, Wes's ability to go from mach ten to, at last, mach zero, never ceased to amaze us.

We marveled and chuckled when we carried him from his car seat into the house . . . laid him on his bed . . . took off his clothes . . . put on his pajamas . . . and put him into his bed without ever waking him up. Even when he was younger, this could all be done including a diaper change.

One evening early in our marriage, Kevin shared with me a highlight of his day at home with Wes.

Apparently, it had started out as a normal day. (I would say "uneventful," but any portion of a day anywhere with Wesley was not ever uneventful.) Wes busied himself with playing and moving, at times playing with the young boy next door. Sometime after lunch, Kevin noticed that the house and yard had become too quiet. He instinctively began looking for his new son. He called and searched the house and yard several times before inquiring with little Lawrence's mom next door.

No, she had not seen Wesley for some time, and Lawrence was with her.

Kevin fought off any panic and calmly, yet thoroughly and quickly, continued his search as any well trained paramedic/fire fighter/search-and-rescue-type father would do. He called Wes's name continually and broadened his search beyond the yard and into the thicket of Russian olive trees behind our home.

No Wes.

Coming back into the yard, Kevin decided to look in the horse trailer, even though it was highly unlikely the child would be in it as the trailer was not rocking and no sounds of activity came from it. Not to mention it would be difficult for a small child to climb into the horse trailer with all the doors shut.

At first glance, the trailer appeared empty, as suspected. Then Kevin saw him.

There, in the feeding loft, curled up and sound asleep was Wesley. With great relief, Kevin picked him up and carried him into the house.

As he finished the recap of his afternoon, Kevin marveled, "I don't know how he slept through my yelling his name like that. The world could be ending, and Wesley would sleep through it."

At age four and five, Wesley's antics like these were mostly considered adorable. Little did we know that these were merely glimpses and just the beginning of what would become a life's pursuit.

The first real behavior problem that got our attention was Wesley's outbursts of anger when being disciplined. At age six, our home and Wes's belongings began suffering damage during disciplining, and his first-grade teacher reported similar problems at school. By the time he was seven, Wesley's second-grade teacher frequented my car window in order to report a current behavioral or academic problem she was having with my son.

I was proud of Wes's enrollment in my church's Christian school. But I was never more embarrassed than the day I was called in to talk to the principal after the school faculty had suffered a difficult "Wesley Day."

I sat in dismay as the principal and teacher reported how his behavior had deteriorated throughout the day and he had required discipline. Wes's teacher advised me of how she had sent him to the gym to do his work as he was distracting the other children in class. Upon checking on him, she found that he had urinated on the gym wall and floor. The principal shared with me his need to suspend Wesley, and not because of the gym incident.

I wanted to sink into the floor when he told me of how Wes had "flipped him off" when he had become involved.

How could this be? I thought. *I have not raised my middle finger to anyone ever in my life and have not seen Kevin make this gesture to anyone. Perhaps it was TV? And why pee on the wall?*

Yet, I believed them. Not just because they were respected adults, but because something inside me knew my son was capable of this kind of behavior.

It had become obvious that disciplining Wesley was a challenge that needed to be quick, effective, and creative.

Praise God for the following four disciplinary tactics that I could not have done without:

Reality Discipline

DAVID WAS NO doubt one of Israel's greatest kings and military leaders. As a ruler he was strong, and he was unsurpassed in his abilities concerning warfare. Yet, he fell terribly short in matters of disciplining his own sons. He responded emotionally, but did not follow through tactically. The result was a family dispute that ended in the death of one son and a futile rebellion ending in the death of another son. David dearly loved his sons. Yet, he seemed not to understand that discipline was also love (2 Samuel 13–15; Hebrews 12:5–6).

Sometime after Wesley's inappropriate behavior at school, I initiated a disciplinary technique God had led me to call Reality Discipline. I discovered the technique in the book *How to Make Your Child Mind Without Losing Yours*, by Dr. Kevin Leman, and adapted it to my needs.

It had been obvious for several years that swats or spankings had not the same effect on Wesley as on some other children. In fact, "the rod" had only proven to be ineffective and most of the time caused an anger reaction that made matters worse. When I began to incorporate Reality Discipline into my dealings with Wes, I found it to be the single, most effective tool in my parenting tool bag, proving successful even into young adulthood.

Reality Discipline is simply using or allowing reality as consequences for negative behavior and as rewards for positive behavior.

For example, when Wesley began a pattern of misbehavior, I would try to remember to say, "Wes, I'm sorry, but our problems this morning have made me tired. I just don't feel like going to the park like we planned. Maybe we can go later if your behavior improves and I feel more rested," instead of, "OK! That's it! No going to the park today!"

Likewise, when Wes had been well behaved or had an improvement in behavior, I would try to remember to say, "Wesley, we have had such a good morning" or "You have made such good changes in your behavior, I feel rested. Let's go to the park!"

After applying this logic only a few times, I also found that many times I could stop the process of negative behavior with a simple warning by saying, "Wes, because of the problems we have been having this morning, I'm starting to feel tired. If we continue to have problems, I'm going to feel too tired to go swimming this afternoon."

If Wes refused to do a chore asked of him, it was much more productive for me when I remembered to say, "Wesley, if you can't clean your room, then I'm going to have to do it. If I do it, we won't have time to stop at the store today."

And again, all were smiles when I could say, "Because you cleaned your room so quickly, we have time to stop at the store so you can spend your allowance. Good job!"

As Wes matured and began to understand social realities, it was even easier. For, if one is disrespectful or hurtful with their actions or words, it's upsetting to the one being disrespected or hurt. The negative consequences are automatic and lingering until amends can be made. This is social reality.

As a mother, social reality meant that if you disrespected me with words or actions, you "ticked me off," and I wasn't going to even THINK about doing anything you wanted.

But remember that at any age, even if just a small dent of an improvement can be noticed in behavior, REWARD—REWARD—REWARD.

There were times that I had to sift through the stress of the day to find the particle of positive behavior that was there. But it WAS there.

Find the positive, act on it, and end every day with it. After all, reality is that at the end of the day something good has always happened.

Time-Outs

REALITY DISCIPLINE AND Time-Outs can work hand in hand and were very effective for us during Wes's younger years. These Reality Time-Outs could be initiated in most any environment.

For example, if Wesley misbehaved in the privacy of our home, I would try to say when calling a time-out, "Go to your room, Wes. What you did/said has upset me. I want to be alone right now. I will call you when I feel better."

If company was in the home at the time, I would sometimes say, "Go to your room, Wes. What you did/said has embarrassed me in front of our friends, and I don't want to be embarrassed."

This was very effective. Even though Wesley might stomp off or be escorted to his room angry, he was quicker to become calm and remorseful when he had been sent to his room with these comments and was less likely to have outbursts during his time-out.

I used time-outs whenever possible. If Wesley's behavior became inappropriate while he was outside, he came in. If he misbehaved in his room, he went to another room or was sat on the couch. Even while at large gatherings in a public area, a simple seat reassignment could be used as a time-out and just a little creativity could turn any time-out into a Reality Time-Out. I had learned and became convinced that it was important to be quick with discipline and to make the discipline short in duration. I learned that responding quickly with these time-outs and resisting the temptation to leave Wesley in one FOREVER was most productive.

I also tried to remember when ending a time-out to say to Wes, "You can come out if you want to" or "You can go when you're ready."

This way, the discipline ended with the privilege to choose instead of a simple release from prison. This could also be easily adapted to other time-out releases.

Removing the Audience

IN ADDITION TO time-outs, a technique called Removing the Audience was very handy. I also learned this technique from Dr. Kevin Leman and Dr. James Dobson. My adaptation to this technique worked well when managing outbursts.

For example, if Wes lost control after being restricted to any location in the house, I would try to go outside where he believed I could not hear his voice or any physical assaults to the house. I would be sure to make my exit obvious to him. If he could not see me leave, I would stop any audible activity that was going on at the time and allow the sound of the front or back door shutting to be the last sound he heard in the house before it became silent. This was almost always effective in limiting the duration of his outburst. If Wesley exhibited a fit while in a public place, I would do my best to walk away. I never had to walk far before he would realize his mother, The Audience, was nowhere near him. It was as if a voice over a PA system had announced, "Ladies and Gentlemen, Wesley's mother has now LEFT THE BUILDING . . . I repeat, Wesley's mother has now LEFT THE BUILDING." Of course, I had only gone around the corner where I could hear him or even see him, camouflaged behind whatever obstacle the establishment had to offer. Although I had to resist the temptation to enhance the scene by spanking my son silly and had to become quite an actress when walking past other people staring at the child I was pretending not to see, the technique worked very well. For it was Wesley who was left to deal with only strangers staring at him and his audience GONE.

Recovery

THE IMPORTANCE OF the well-being of children and the taking of time to comfort and bless them is strongly expressed by our Lord.

During the time that Jesus walked the earth, it was also common for adults to feel overwhelmed with day-to-day matters and miss opportunities to interact lovingly with children. Jesus showed us all that nothing is more important than comforting, blessing, and lovingly touching our children (Matthew 19:13–15).

This can be especially challenging when parents are overwhelmed with dealing with negative behaviors and the need to discipline.

I cannot find the words to begin to express the importance of recovery after discipline for any child, and even more so for the child with ADHD. It is crucial that a parent allows as much time as their child needs for this. It is absolutely imperative that every child is given the opportunity to know that he/she is forgiven, is a good child, that your love is unconditional, and that you, yourself, are not perfect. Recovery following discipline must occur on the child's time when he/she is ready.

Some parent personalities struggle with this. Some parents find themselves needing time for their own recovery before they are able to interact lovingly with a child that has recently misbehaved and is ready for recovery. If you are this type of personality, my advice to you is this:

Get over it!

Get on with it!

And for heaven's sake, SNAP OUT OF IT!

A beautiful door is closing while you pout. Most children are naturals at forgiving and forgetting the mistakes of their parents. Who are we to deny them the same?

During Wesley's young years, he typically was ready for recovery soon after a problem and discipline had taken place. It wasn't hard to read him and know when the time was right. Even when very young, he was an excellent communicator. With a look, body language, or words, he would let me know just how he felt. When he was ready, Wes would either initiate or respond to a hug or being held. It was during this time that he was most receptive to talking about the recent course of events. And it was also during this time that he was most ready to absorb my reassurance that he was not a bad child and that there was nothing he could do to lose my love. Recovery time was an excellent opportunity for me to mirror the way Jesus loves us all.

At times, however, recovery was painful.

For example, when Wes lost a privilege such as going to the park or swimming due to his behavior, part of his recovery time was spent in remorse and crying, begging for the privilege to be returned to him. Hang in there! This is a necessary grieving process. Wesley always eventually came to terms with his loss and almost always became determined to change his behavior and re-earn the privilege.

No matter how long it takes, take the time for a full recovery.

I believe these techniques were largely responsible for our many moments of successful day-to-day management of Wesley, and that they can be applied to any child.

Most of all, remember the importance of being quick to respond with discipline and keep its duration short. Look for every opportunity to reward and make a Big Deal out of any positive behavior, no matter how minuscule it may seem. Take notice of, and take time to embrace, every moment of these absolutely endearing years.

2

Ages 8-11

"Wow, how he's grown . . . What is he doing? . . . Oh no!"

BY THE TIME Wesley was eight, we had been living on our 2½ acre bit of heaven for about two years. Wes and the two brothers living next to us had become inseparable and made good use of the half-acre pond, floating dock, tree house, and the stream running through the adjoining properties in the wooded area below. Their mother, Penny, and I had also become best friends, and we enjoyed doing things together with the boys. Penny's son, Daelin, was just a few months older than Wes, and her youngest son, Colin, was a year and a half younger. Needless to say, my friend and I found ourselves sharing in the parenting of quite a threesome. I finally understood the strange phrase my grandmother quoted so many times.

"One boy—all boy . . . two boys—half a boy . . . three boys—no boy at all."

What one boy wouldn't think of to do, one of the others would. And what two boys didn't know how to do, the one that did would show the other two how to do it. As a result, no idea was left unthought of or untried.

Penny and I would call each other frequently to discuss the boys, where they were, and what they were doing, or to make plans and chat. And every so often there was a phone call that was unforgettable.

It was a typical fall weekend day.

Wesley, Colin, and Daelin had spent the day playing and going back and forth to each other's homes as they always did. It wasn't too difficult to keep up with them. A certain level of noise always accompanied the boys and made for a good homing device. Even above the sound of the running water of the stream through the trees and over the hilly terrain, their voices could be heard as they swam and fished, hunted crayfish and built forts. Whenever the area became too quiet, Penny and I would give each other a call or go looking for our triplets when necessary. This particular afternoon became one of those.

I had not yet noticed the alarming silence until the phone rang. As I answered it, the realization of silence hit me.

"Hello."

"Jan," Penny's voice said with the sound of restrained laughter. "Have you looked in your backyard at the pond?"

"Not recently."

She giggled.

"Uh, I think you should take a look."

I held the phone to my ear as I walked out the back door onto the porch. As I surveyed the area, I noticed many little white "things" floating and littering the pond. Also hanging from and ornamenting several surrounding trees were many more little white things.

"What on earth . . ." I uttered.

"I think they got into Melissa's stuff."

"Melissa's stuff . . ."

(Melissa was Penny's teenage daughter.) At last I came close enough to understand Penny's phone call. All the many little white things were opened TAMPONS. They were everywhere!

"There're tampons!" I exclaimed.

"I know. I think they used the whole box. I'm trying not to laugh, but it's funny to me."

I laughed.

"It IS funny. Why are you trying not to laugh?"

"Well, you're not going to like what they tried to do to Ponchy."

She was right. I became furious when she told me of how one of my dogs (male) had become involved in the fun. I was ready to string up three boys in the trees!

Thankfully the dog was smart enough to get away from them and had not been harmed and as time went on I also found the humor in the incident. It became one of many Penny and I laughed about when reminiscing through the years. However, I can tell you that it was on The Day of the Tampons the "fear of Jan's wrath" was instilled in the boys.

After this the phrase, "You mess with one of Jan's animals, you DIE," became well known.

Because Kevin and I worked full time for the local ambulance service and were on different shifts, we had equal exposure to the antics of The Three Musketeers.

When Colin, Wes, and Daelin were about ages eight, nine, and ten, Kevin found himself sensing the need to check on the boys as a peace and tranquility had settled for too long. Stepping outside, he found all to be quiet. Too quiet. Kevin walked past the pond and stood on the dam, calling down the hill toward the stream. But all that called back was a breeze rustling the leaves of the trees and the sound of the rushing water. Then, in the far distance, Kevin thought he heard their voices shouting in play. He followed the sound. Upon locating the boys, Kevin found them precariously dangling many feet above the stream over a sandstone drop-off on BAILING TWINE. Upon further investigation, he discovered that the three had tied many pieces of twine together to create a repelling rope and had tied it off on a small bush growing out of the side of the steep, sandy hill above the drop-off. They then tied themselves to the twine by their belts and belt loops.

Repelling on bailing twine is something a child just shouldn't do when their father is Safety God (the loving nickname Kevin earned). But instead of being a party-pooping parent and taking away the children's fun, Kevin was gracious enough to take the time to equip the boys with real repelling equipment, hands-on instruction, and a set of strict rules. After The Twine Repelling Incident, Colin, Wes, and Daelin spent many days enjoying low-angle repelling off the various hills near our home. As for their parents, we just prayed.

I was well acquainted with the power of prayer early in life. But I became more and more experienced with it with each passing year of my son's life.

Upon reflection, it is evident that prayer was the only true power I ever had.

Even a very safety conscious father like Kevin found he was powerless to protect his son all of the time. Neither of us had felt more powerless than we did on a snow-covered mountain near our home one winter morning.

It was Wesley's first ski trip ever, my first in many years, and Kevin's first in a few years. We were joining Wes and his fellow students for a school ski trip. It was a beautiful clear day, and our group was busting with excitement. Young Wesley had been skiing with the instructors on the teaching hill all morning and was bubbling over with confidence as he rode the chair lift higher up the mountain for the first time.

His confidence was not completely undeserved. Wes was very coordinated and learned new physical skills quickly.

We exited the chair lift and skied a short distance to the crest of a mild ski slope. As Kevin and I gathered ourselves in preparation to flank Wesley on the way down, little Wes pointed his skies downhill and was off before we even knew what had happened. It became immediately evident that whether his quick start was an accident or not, there was soon going to be one. With each gaining yard, Wesley fought harder and harder for balance. Kevin skied after him with grace and speed as I followed behind with less of each.

We both yelled out to Wes, "Make a wedge! Make a pie! Stop . . . Stop!"

But to no avail. He continued clumsily down the hill, leaning over on one ski, then the other as he narrowly missed trees and other skiers, all the while gaining dangerous speed. Before I was halfway down the mountain, Wesley descended a second hill and disappeared from sight with Kevin skiing hard to catch him. All I could do was pray for angels to protect my little out-of-control skier. By the time I reached the bottom of the run, I found Kevin stopped, craning his neck to look about the lifts and ski resort buildings.

My mind went crazy, "Where is Wes?"

We quickly skied beyond the buildings toward the parking lots. There we found him. Frozen in his tracks (quite literally), Wesley had come to rest precariously on the edge of a fifteen -foot drop-off above a parking lot with his skies only half on the edge.

Some may have speculated, "He simply ran out of momentum just in time." But I knew better.

Angels were surrounding my son. They always did, and they always would.

These years were full of incidents like these. From pan-frying fishing worms (don't ask) to attempting to drive the car out of the garage while wearing rollerblades (a manual transmission), Wesley kept us hopping, praying, and laughing.

As is true with the rearing of any child, ages eight through eleven presents new and changing challenges for parents of children with ADHD.

Find a Middle Ground

DURING THESE YEARS I came to understand that Reality Discipline, Time-Outs, Removing the Audience, and Recovery were the foundation of my management techniques when dealing with negative behavior. And even more important, the realization that God MUST be the cornerstone began to sink in deeper. ANYTIME ANYTHING my husband and I did turned out productive concerning Wes was when we allowed God to guide my instincts and Kevin's detailed and logical mind.

It has often been said, "What a man THINKS, a woman FEELS."

God knows this perfectly. It is He who designed it this way. When parents are praying for their children and for guidance in raising them, God uses these natural avenues to communicate with them.

When I listened to God as He influenced my instincts and my husband's reasoning, the result was always very good. However, finding the middle ground where God would have us in order to hear Him clearly was difficult. Because Kevin and I were the Poster Parents for each extreme, finding the middle message was often stressful and exhausting. There were times that I could find the energy to work with Kevin through a Wesley Challenge and come up with something we could both live with. Other times, I had not an ounce of energy left in my deepest resources. Kevin, on the other hand, seemed to have an endless supply.

This is a common problem for parents and is not gender specific. It creates challenges in the rearing of any child and has numerous negative effects. Parents find themselves thinking independently of each other, struggling for dominance, and spending precious time trying to prove each other wrong.

STOP!

The last thing any child needs is separated parents. This applies to parents who are already not living in the same house. No matter the situation, if two share in the parenting of a child, it is imperative that they be seen as ONE in the best interest of that child. Ah, but being "one in the best interest" does not mean that parents must win each other over to the other's way of thinking. In fact, it usually means quite the opposite.

It is absolutely OK for parents to agree to disagree when discussing what they think is best for their child, as long as they are both able to live with the final decision made concerning that child. For most parents, a decision of this type lies somewhere in the middle. It is of great importance that parents take the time and energy needed to accomplish these agreements. Because of this, it is of even GREATER importance that parents learn to budget and restore their energy.

Energy Budgeting

GOD'S EXAMPLE AND then command of purposely setting aside time for rest and recuperation is noted many times throughout the Bible. The creation of the Sabbath Day and the Lord's directions on how to keep it are designed to cause His people to do what we are not very good at doing on our own—to balance work with rest and gain rejuvenation from time spent with Him (Genesis 2:2–3; Exodus 20:8–11).

Contrary to what most children believe, parents do not come assigned to them with an endless supply of money or energy. Likewise, many parents are surprised when they find themselves suffering from Superparent Syndrome and their energy account balance in the red. An energy deficit stops all productivity, creates frustration and friction between parents, and causes inconsistencies for the child. In the case of Wesley's parents, it was I who suffered most from the syndrome caused by a depleted energy supply.

Like many parents, Kevin and I were very different in many ways. Kevin cared about many issues concerning Wes. I cared about some issues. And the degree of importance we each put on issues we both cared about was off by double digits. At times, this produced a nice balance as we each influenced the other to look at things from a different perspective. However, this balance took energy. Kevin seemed to have plenty, as if he were tapped into an unseen energy supply. I, on the other hand, had only what God had given me at birth and required more deposits.

I was born an optimist and a nurturer, a lover of all things, creatures and all people, and a finder of good in everything with no sense of awareness of detail. Kevin was born a thinker, a planner, an avoider, and solver of problems with a heightened sense and awareness of detail. As a result, sharing parenting between us was equally draining, my supply of energy simply running out long before Kevin's did.

Due to our differences and the nearing of Wesley's preteen years, I came to accept the fact that I must spend my energy wisely. I had no other choice. It was a matter of survival. I had to know my strengths as well as my limitations. I had to admit my weaknesses and learn how to draw strength from God. I had to be HONEST. No more codependent—sugarcoating—avoiding conflict—"don't want to be mean" way of thinking. I had to be honest with myself, my children and their friends, my husband, and our parents and friends.

Thankfully, God made this fairly easy for me. All I had to do was trust my instincts, my gut. If I felt strongly about an issue concerning Wesley, I knew it was worth taking whatever time and energy it needed. If I didn't feel strongly about an issue or idea presented to me, I knew I should spend some time and energy listening to other's opinions with an open mind. And if I felt strongly opposed to an issue, idea, or technique presented to me, I knew it demanded an EXPLOSION of energy. But here's the bottom line. No matter the situation, I also had to understand that I must be REAL.

Before making any decision of any kind, I had to ask myself, "What is the reality? Can I do this? Can I carry this out? Can I support this idea?" Then I had to answer myself honestly.

Restoring Energy

DAVID'S 23RD PSALM is one of the most quoted and misused Bible passages by the secular world. So many times it is seen associated with death and despair, and yet, the psalmist wrote it as just the opposite. David felt safe, rested, and refreshed because of his relationship with the Lord that he relates to as a sheep to his shepherd. He understood the need to restore his body and spirit. The Bible is full of this teaching through the experience of many of its writers. God gives precise directions on how to find our rest as spoken by the words of Jesus. And He, Himself, often took the opportunity to rest from His work and retreat from the people and His disciples when going up on the mountain to spend time with the Father (Psalm 23: 1-3, Matthew 11:28-30, Matthew 14:22–23).

Marriage, parenting, and work are life accomplishments that can be very positive. God can bless us with these as they give us a sense of achievement, pride, and happiness. But they are, no doubt, daily energy drainers. In addition, other outside stresses are guaranteed to come our way.

It is no secret that energy out must, at least, equal energy in. I learned this the hard way.

My father was an anchor in my life. He and I shared not only the same birthday but a special father-daughter bond. No matter how old I became , I was his "little girl" and he was my "daddy." He was witty, silly, and smart, with a wonderful mixture of a good-ole-country-boy and a sophisticated modern man. Daddy raised me to feel intelligent and strong and to be assertive when needed. He was not perfect but was the laughter of my life. My father suffered from emphysema for many years and died when Wesley was eleven. This left a gaping hole in my being that I could not explain. On the outside, I was charging on with stoic strength and even emotions. But even I did not understand what was happening on the inside.

In the 5 years that followed my father's death, I also lost my grandfather; my mentor—my mother; my more-than-best friend who taught me of Jesus; and my grandmother, my spirit. Each loss only added to the pit of emptiness I carried in my core, sapping me of precious energy. I looked like a rock on the outside. But on the inside, I was lying in an exhausted heap.

My story is like so many. "A person fearlessly charging through life with 100 percent passion, taking care of everyone while taking on the world, finds he/she has forgotten to take care of himself/herself." And I did what many hurting and exhausted people do. I found comfort and a source of energy in the wrong place and with the wrong thing. In reality, this gave only a temporary escape that left me emptier and even more exhausted with every turn; the typical destructive by-products of a developing or existing dependency. How could a well brought up Christian girl not turn to God for comfort and to restore her energy? If it hasn't happened to you, then you will have to take my word for it: TOO EASILY.

Praise God for His wisdom, His patience, His forgiveness, and His love. Through it all, God never left me, just as He promised. He taught me the necessity of restoring my energy through time spent with Him as well as other important God-given avenues, many of which are simple requirements for a healthy mind and body that we foolishly deny ourselves.

Sleep

ALONG WITH THE physical need for the body to rest, the mind must also rest.

God chose to create our brains with the need to recharge. One might think this was a bit lazy on the Creator's part. But our need to sleep is more than it appears on the surface. It is our need to dream that not only recharges us but also allows for reception of God's communication with us (Job 33:14–18).

Christian dream interpretation is well studied by many, and more can be learned from those well versed in the area of hearing the Lord's voice through dreams.

Jesus, after becoming like us, also had to recharge His mind with sleep.

Multitudes of people with great physical and spiritual needs pressed about Him continually. On one recorded occasion, the Lord recognized His need to remove Himself from the people and sleep. He directed the disciples to man boats so that they all could take to sea and cross to the other side for much-needed rest. Sometime later while at sea, Jesus' sleep was so deep that He had to be awakened by the frightened disciples when a storm had ensued (Matthew 8:18, 23–26).

So stop kidding yourself. YOU MUST SLEEP. The dishes can wait. The clutter is not going anywhere. You can get by without that load of laundry tonight. And you are not a bad parent if you tell your children, their friends, and the cousins, "No sleepover tonight."

Most sleep authorities recommend eight hours of uninterrupted sleep every day. Of course, everyone is different. Some adults require more. Some people do not seem to need as much. But all human beings have to sleep in order to restore energy and recharge their minds and bodies. I believe parents are some of the most consistently sleep-deprived individuals, and that the parents of children with ADHD top the list.

The only way to ensure adequate sleep is to PRIORITIZE it. Bump it up there! Obviously, sleeping requires opportunity. But it is we who are responsible for stopping the grind and seizing the opportunity. The easiest way to seize opportunity is to make opportunity. Just as you enforce a bedtime for your children, enforce one for yourself. Establish a bedtime and keep it. Also, if you don't already, practice a bedtime routine. Whatever it is that relaxes you before bed, take the time to do it. If you have serious trouble sleeping, seek medical attention.

Also remember to listen to your body. Regardless of how much sleep you thought you got the night before, if you feel tired TAKE A NAP. A thirty-minute nap may be all you need.

Sleeping is a natural energy restorer. It is of vital importance that you sleep and sleep well.

Eat

OH BOY! FOOD can be a touchy subject. There are already more than enough gurus out there to confuse and complicate the natural and simple concept of feeding ourselves. And I have no secret wonder diet that will give you endless energy, wisdom, and weight loss. The last thing the parent of a challenging child needs is to stress over what they should eat.

Even in its perfect form before the fall of mankind, the human body was designed to use food to sustain it. The Lord created us to not only need food but to enjoy it. Our minds are stimulated by the pleasurable tastes and textures as we eat and as our body absorbs nutrients into every cell, giving us energy for function and performance (Genesis 1:29; 2:9).

Everyone is different and approaches food differently. There is no absolute right or wrong way to eat. The only absolute is that we must do it. It is a known fact that without good nutrition the body and mind cannot function properly. Nutritionists and dietitians will always be able to advise us on how to properly balance our food intake. And there is certainly nothing wrong with following professionally approved guidelines. But believe it or not, our body actually knows what it needs. Listen to it. When you feel hungry, EAT. Eat what sounds good to you. If a pickle, mustard, and potato chip sandwich would "just hit the spot" . . . EAT IT. Then stop when you are full. If a bowl of applesauce filled you up, STOP EATING. Likewise, if you polish off an entire steak, baked potato, and veggies, plus dessert before you became satisfied, THAT'S OK. When one becomes proficient at hearing what their body has to say, they will find themselves well nourished, less stressed, and more content.

When I followed this simplified approach to eating, I found that my body asked for nutritious food and told me when it was satisfied. As a result, I was blessed with more energy and felt less stressed.

Discover more information about simplified eating and a healthy relationship with food by researching author and workshop creator and speaker Geneen Roth.

Exercise

OK, I'M GOING to spend very little time on this topic. Everyone knows the benefits of regular exercise. There is no magic. Our bodies were designed for movement, agility, and ability. Exercise does many good things for the human body on many levels. Find whatever physical activity it is that you enjoy doing and JUST DO IT. Once again, prioritize it. You don't have to beat yourself for hours every day. A simple brisk walk, thirty minutes a day, is of great benefit any time of year. During seasonal weather, tending outdoor gardens and yards is a wonderful and rewarding way to exercise the body (Genesis 2:5, 15).

Some parents have jobs that are more physically demanding, as was the case with me. But do not allow this to replace regular exercise.

In addition, embrace the blessing of keeping up with your active child. Play with him/her. Run—jump—dance—swing—slide—ride—climb—swim—ski—skate—sled. Children with ADHD know how to have fun! Being physically fit, active, and having fun are guaranteed energy boosters.

Time For Yourself—Rest

GOD NOT ONLY understood the need to direct His people to take a day of rest, He also knew that He must teach them to plan for it and prioritize it. I think the Lord had parents in mind when He did this. The Sabbath was made so that we might take time for ourselves! (Exodus 16:23; Leviticus 23:3)

This is the concept I struggled most with. Because I was a nurturer, I tended to focus more on pleasing other people rather than myself. I, like many parents, put my needs aside so that I could take care of the needs of my children, family, and friends.

The stress of raising a child who had ADHD with a detail-oriented husband, the deaths of my father and grandparents, as well as my mother's illness and death, obviously took a toll on me. It would anybody. But my response to these stresses, no matter how sensible it seemed at first, only set me up for disaster later. Instead of admitting my needs and turning to what could take care of them, I reasoned that the only way to avoid the additional stress and frustration of disappointment was to let go. And I mean LET GO. That's what I did. I perfected the art. I let go of my husband and my friends, my horses, my music, and my writing. Worst of all, I felt too busy to spend much time with the Lord or to recognize the Sabbath for its true purpose. And all the while, I was letting go of people through death who were dear to me. It was as if I took the act of letting go of lost loved ones and applied it across the board. I held on to only my children. THAT WAS IT.

It later became obvious to me the importance of hanging onto God and the people and things in life that nurtured, fed, and energized me. Through hard learned lessons, I realized the need to admit and communicate with my husband, family, and friends what I needed from them. I came to understand the necessity of allowing myself time to spend with God in prayer and devotional reading, to commune with my church family and make music, to be active with my horses and to write. And I became reacquainted with the Sabbath and its endless benefits.

I am convinced that I did not suffer the Letting Go Affliction alone. I believe there are many who know what I'm talking about. Yet, there are some who are better at allowing themselves time to do things they enjoy. And some people are TOO good at taking care of #1. Once again, there is a happy medium, that wonderful place in our daily existence that is so difficult to find. But it is imperative that each day we make the attempt to find it. If we make the attempt, we are likely to, at least, come close. When we do this, our energy cup runneth over.

Whether we were prepared for it or not, Wesley's teen years sprang upon us from around a corner. It was time to fasten our seat belts and hang on! Our little roller-coaster ride was about to become a THRILLER.

3

Ages 12-15

"He's a creative kid . . . What on earth . . . You have got to be kidding me!"

IT WAS A warm, late-spring day. The sky was clear and blue, and choirs of birds sang gaily. Our rooster, Elvis, was crooning to the hens as they clucked back in approval. The rabbits were busy digging in the dirt floor of the coop, and Big Mamma rabbit was making a welcome nest in the henhouse alongside a sitting hen, they both expecting soon arrivals. The dogs were playing a game of chase in the backyard, and the barn kittens were batting at butterflies in the front yard. The horses were sunbathing on the ground, taking their morning siesta. The kingfisher and heron had returned to the pond and were perched at their strategic locations as the fish jumped at the gnats unawares. The doors and windows of the house were open, inviting all inside while I busied about the daily chores. The children were already out-side, and I was anxious to join them in outdoor activities. Jami was playing on the enclosed back deck, and the distant voices of the boys playing not far away could be heard. It was one of those moments in time when all felt good. No one was sick. No one was fighting or in trouble. No one needed a nap, and no issues were in need of address-ing at the time. All was well.

Suddenly, the voices of the boys became excited and quickly

drew nearer to the house. I heard six shoes stomp up the back steps and turned to see Wesley, Colin, and Daelin filing in through the open sliding glass door. They were shirtless, clad only in blue jeans— and were covered in BLOOD. Only a few specs of clean skin could be found on their faces. There was even blood in their hair.

Perhaps my on-the-job training as a mom is what kept me calm. Or, it could have been my training and experience as an EMT that caused me to stand back and assess the scene before acting. Maybe it was just common sense that told me that it couldn't be their blood that I was seeing.

But nothing could keep my mouth from uttering, "What in the hell!" (I should have said, "What on earth!" but in all honesty, I didn't.)

"Mom, it was so cool! We dissected a raccoon!" Wes said with excitement.

"What!"

"Yeah, we killed it with my blowgun dart ," Daelin said proudly.

"And we took its brains out and everything!" Wes added. "We have to rinse off because we were throwing guts at each other."

"Yeah, Wes threw some at me, and it went in my mouth," Colin said in his quiet, calm voice.

"You have *got* to be kidding me!" I said with some surprise but mostly disgust. "I can't believe you killed a harmless raccoon! How did you get close enough to kill it with blow darts?"

"Don't worry, Jan." Daelin said in a reassuring voice. "It was on our property, and we think it was real sick."

"Oh great, you boys just became ONE with a diseased raccoon. Get your butts in the shower right now!" I ordered sternly.

While the boys showered, I made the inevitable phone call to Penny. After explaining all that I had just learned, she and I decided to go see their experiment. Behind Penny's garage we discovered a crude, outdoor lab. The remains of what used to be a raccoon were strewn across an old, long, folding table along with rusted knives, saws, and screwdrivers. Blood smeared the table and soaked spots along the ground. It looked more like a scene from a bad horror film.

We fully expected to find a mutilated mutant swinging from a chain when we rounded the corner.

Over the next few days, Penny and I discussed the recent event. She had suspected all along that Daelin's blowgun was actually considered a weapon and that the boys, being minors, were not legally able to possess one. After checking with the local sheriff's department, she found it to be true and had a deputy take the gun from her son and talk with all three boys about the significance of the infraction. (A little mom-inspired scare tactic. It worked.) Penny and I also became concerned about the animal possibly having rabies and wondered if it were possible for the boys to contract the disease without being bitten. Penny researched information on the Internet and discovered that in the state of New Mexico, raccoons were second only to bats for carrying rabies and that there had not been a reported case of a rabid raccoon in many years. We talked with our local Game and Fish Department authorities who informed us that the only way the boys could possibly contract the disease was if they scratched their skin with the animal's teeth, as rabies would have been carried in the saliva. They told us that the animal could be tested for rabies if we were able to package it's skull with at least some brain tissue intact and send it in for testing.

By this time, the boys had become frightened and wanted us to test the animal. We packaged the skull as instructed and waited for the results. While waiting, Wesley became especially worried while Colin and Daelin became less worried as did and Penny and I. The authorities had advised us that the probability of the boys contracting rabies was highly unlikely. When the test came back inconclusive due to lack of brain tissue, a frightened Wes insisted that he receive the series of rabies shots he would need to ensure he did not get "sick and die." This was done as he requested for his peace of mind.

Since the Raccoon Dissection Incident, I continue to be the only parent I know who has had their child vaccinated for rabies . . . just as a precaution.

I'm sure all parents would be interested in a vaccination that would protect their children from harm as soon as they start driving.

My father, being the son of a Texas cotton farmer that he was, had my brothers and me behind the wheel of a car as soon as we could see over the dash. We learned to steer a car early in life, sitting on his lap as we putted along old dirt roads or on the quiet street where we lived in the city. (Understand that this was before seat belt laws, laws against riding in the back of trucks or campers, and safe child seat restraints—although I don't think these would have stopped him.) As soon as we could reach the pedals, we were enrolled in Daddy's Driving School. On these same roads he insisted we learn to drive a manual transmission vehicle, learn to pull and back a trailer, and to parallel park a car of any size. As a result, by the time we were licensed to drive we were quite accomplished at driving and had an understanding of defensive driving as well. Not surprisingly, I carried on this tradition with my children.

Once we arrived at our trail of choice, I would turn the wheel over to Wesley or one of the other older drivers-in-training, and then I'd enjoy the beautiful scenery from the backseat with the younger children. I would require the vehicle to stop regularly to allow the younger girls to get out and pick wildflowers in the meadows. Packed with us was always a mean picnic basket that we enjoyed emptying when we found an interesting place to stop and eat and enjoy some exploring. Our goal was to be off the mountain by dark, where I would take over the wheel and drive us all home, enjoying the best sound in the entire world . . . the sound of a vehicle full of sleeping children.

I'm sure by this time it is not hard for one to believe that not all of Wes's driving experiences were like the one just described. He went through many vehicles. (Not all his fault.)

His first vehicle was the family miniwagon, a small manual transmission vehicle. Its only misfortune was a dented front bumper and damaged radiator when Wes, at age ten, tried to back it out of the garage wearing roller blades and nearly pinning Daelin to a support beam.

A Toyota 4Runner replaced this vehicle for practical reasons. The 4Runner was not ever damaged. However, it WAS the vehicle that ran over Daelin's knee when he ran toward the truck (driven by Wesley) as it pulled into the driveway while he tried to strike at Colin who verbally offended him from the passenger's seat. This vehicle was also replaced due to a failing ignition and low power.

Wes's next vehicle was a full-size Blazer. Today, if you could find this Blazer were it was laid to rest in a junkyard, it would tell quite a story with its twisted body—missing windshield—broken roof—and shattered side windows. It would tell a story about a boy, his absent-minded mother, his cousin, and their guardian angels.

It was a beautiful day in the high desert. The children and I had planned an off-road driving trip about the bluffs, canyon, and small lake near our home. As was NOT common, I had only Wes and my nephew, Chris, with me. Jami had stayed with my brother, Bill and his wife, Cindy, so she could play with her cousin, Sarah, Chris's sister. We were also blessed that day to have one of my fellow paramedic partners and good friend, Julian, join us. He planned on rendezvous-ing with us, and his contribution to our outing had the boys very excited. Julian loved and collected guns. I had a small .38 revolver (a gift from my gun-loving grandfather), and we had decided to do a little target shooting somewhere along the way. Julian was excellent with children, especially teenage boys, and I appreciated his willing-ness to teach gun safety to Wes and Chris.

After meeting Julian and arriving at the long dirt road that led through the canyon, I turned the wheel over to Wes and got in the passenger's seat of my friend's truck so we could chat as we led the boys along the roadways. The outing was going wonderfully. The bluffs topped with piñon, cedar, and pine trees reached to the heav-ens, and so did we as we climbed among them. We stopped to eat, explore, and to shoot the guns.

Julian was a brazen, somewhat intimidating British man who in-stantly had the attention and respect of Wes and Chris. He took his role as gun instructor very seriously, but also showed the boys a great time. When it was time to make the slow trek toward the highway and then home, we all jumped in the vehicles the same way we came. Only this time, I allowed Christopher to take the wheel of the Blazer as had been promised him earlier in the day.

Chris was younger than Wes, but was nearly Wesley's size and had done some driving. Bill had also been doing for his boy what our father had done for us. So when we descended the bluffs and reached the wide dirt road in the canyon, Christopher proudly jumped in the driver's seat.

Julian and I led the way, chatting about this and that. This came naturally to us. We had been sitting in an ambulance together as partners for more than ten years. What we didn't realize was that, just as it was for us at work, we were waiting for the next catastrophe.

We had nearly completed the eight-mile drive along the canyon road. Julian and I had not any worries about this road. It was wide and flat with mostly open fields on either side. As we rounded the S curves near the top of the road, Julian and I suddenly became aware that the boys had fallen back and were not behind us. My friend slowed his truck. Still, there was no sign of them coming around the bend.

Julian stopped. "Where are they?" he asked.

"I don't know. Julian, they were right behind us just moments ago," I replied.

"I know. I've been watching them. They were there just before we started the turns." Julian turned his truck around, and we began driving back around the bends in the road.

As we rounded the second turn, our hearts sank. Walking on the road was Wesley, his hand bleeding.

My breath left me. "Where's Chris? Where's the Blazer?"

As we reached Wes we were able to see the top of the Blazer where it had come to rest on its wheels in the only ravine for ten miles. Our experience and instincts told us that it had rolled and that the possibility for injury was high.

"Oh, Mom . . ." Wes said fighting back tears, "Dad's going to be so mad! We rolled my Blazer! Oh, he's going to be mad!"

"Wes, where's Christopher?" I said. My mind was spinning with flashbacks of calls at work.

"He's in the ravine. He's OK. He's climbing out."

"I'm right here, Aunt Jan," Chris called out, his arms and head coming into view as he climbed up to the road.

Julian and I checked the boys over. They seemed to have only superficial cuts and abrasions. We learned that Chris had been ejected, along with the windshield that was lying in the dirt near where the vehicle landed, and that Wes had remained in the vehicle but ended up in the back of it.

This put my already-self-blame into high gear. "Why did I not check to be sure they were wearing their seat belts? I usually do. And most of the time, they already would have them on. Why didn't I this time? Why didn't they? They could have been killed! Oh, Lord Jesus, thank you. Thank you, Jesus," I prayed.

As I called Bill and Cindy to let them know what had happened, Julian phoned some of our fellow rescue friends to come assist us in pulling the Blazer from the ravine. I also phoned my husband who was at work, to update him on the event. I knew Kevin would not be upset about the vehicle but only worried about the boys. Kevin talked to Wes and reassured him of this. After two hours of numerous attempts by numerous friends to pull the Blazer out, my brother arrived at the scene with a flatbed trailer and a buddy. Within five minutes he had managed to start the vehicle and demand it to back itself over the boulders, bushes, and trees, up the steep hill, and out onto the road. Its bent axles and flat tires had not hindered Bill the way they had the rest of us. With the help of my friends and their equipment, the vehicle recovery was complete. Then my brother loaded the beaten Blazer onto the flatbed and within twenty minutes we all drove home.

For years Christopher was teased about his driving capabilities. But we all knew who was responsible for the accident: Aunt Jan. We also knew who was responsible for the protection of two boys that day: God.

After the rollover incident, Wesley and Chris became avid seat belt wearers with a new respect for kinetic energy. I too became a little less passive that day.

While adventures like these were going on at home during Wesley's early teen year, adventures of another kind were going on at school.

Wes was no stranger to problems as school due to behavioral infractions. It was not unusual in our house to receive regular phone calls from the school. The public school in our area was very good about keeping parents apprised of any behavioral problems their child was having and any disciplinary action the school had taken. These calls were frequent, frustrating, and almost desensitizing. More times than not, the calls would catch me already exhausted since behavioral problems at school paralleled similar problems at home.

It was hard for me not to interrupt a teacher's report by saying, "You know what? I really just don't want to know. You took care of it. It has nothing to do with me. My watch doesn't start until 4:00 p.m. I AM NOT ON DUTY RIGHT NOW. YOUR ARE! Get some coffee, eat some chocolate, and do some deep breathing exercises. You'll be fine."

Unfortunately, school suspensions were nearly as regular as the phone calls and could not be taken lightly. Suspensions were the result of a problem going beyond the school's ability to deal with it. For me, these days were some of the most challenging. No matter how callused repetition may have caused me to be, it was hard to ignore the impact of my child's behavior when the school had no other alternative than to have the truancy officer bring him home.

There were then (and will always be) people who, after hearing about this kind of problem with a young person, write the teen off as "never amount to anything," "a failure," "worthless," or "a strain on society."

They are WRONG. I guarantee it. The young person with ADHD has just as much potential for success in life as anyone else. In addition (this is heavy), parents have the power to lift, guide, and strengthen them along their journey or shatter them before they can even begin.

Attitude Is Where It's At (The Power of Positive Thinking)

A POSITIVE ATTITUDE is one of the most powerful instruments a parent can possess. With it one can annihilate tension—destroy doubt—arrest an argument—bar depression—lift spirits—change moods—nurture faith—and yes—even MOVE MOUNTAINS. Best of all, IT IS CONTAGIOUS and spreads quickly.

God deserves all the glory for creating in me a positive spirit. It was He who made this to come naturally for me. I am so fortunate for this blessing. Positive thinking is not a natural state of mind or personality trait that everyone has. Yet, it does have drawbacks. People like me tend to overlook reality and can miss crucial signs of a possible problem. However, I believe God allowed me the gift of optimism for reasons I am still discovering. The most important and obvious reasons being for the raising of the two children He gave to me as well as for the nurturing of the children that filled our home. I have seen the magic of a positive attitude work in my life. The benefits have spilled over into my relationships with friends, coworkers, and other acquaintances as well.

If your personality tends to be more guarded, do not worry. A small amount of optimism goes a long way and is very valuable. Even positive people have their seasons of negative thinking and need a little spirit lift. I found this simple, three-step exercise to be helpful during negative moments and when coaching a beloved pessimist:

AS SOON AS POSSIBLE, STOP—Assess the situation and find ONE good thing about it or that could result from it. Even if you are not able to do this until sometime after the fact, that is OK. The more you practice, the more efficient you will become at quickly finding something positive in any situation.

VERBALIZE WHAT YOU FOUND—As soon as the timing seems right, share your positive thought. If possible, be certain your teenager is one of the first to hear it. If what you have to say is about your teen personally, confess your optimism about him/her in their presence and in the presence of others. When this is not possible, tell your child about your plans to share what you think with certain others, and then follow through. If your teenager has a negative attitude, then it is even simpler. Seize the right moment and let him/her know about the good that you see.

PRAISE GOD—Thank God for His wisdom, power, and love, and then TELL YOUR TEEN about it. Let him/her know how much God loves them, how happy you are that He has given them to you, and how much you love them. If the negative situation is due to another person, apply this fact about God to that person in the presence of your child. If a negative challenge is due to an event, remind yourself of God's infinite wisdom in all situations, and then share this fact with your teenager.

It is a known fact that positive people draw others to them for obvious reasons. Likewise, teenagers are drawn to positive parents. Practice a positive attitude and watch the magic happen right before your eyes (Proverbs 15:13–15, 30; 17:22).

Teens and Stress

DAVID WAS NO stranger to stress. While still a young man, he not only was aware of the intensity of his future as king, but experienced life as a fugitive for years due to the jealous and insecure King Saul who tirelessly pursued him in order to kill him. And I can think of no greater stress than for a king to have to deal with a significant rebellion led by his own son. Yet the Psalms are full of the peace David experienced while under these stressful times (Psalm 3; Psalm 54; Psalm 144).

Jesus also reminded the disciples that simple faith would ward off stress and worry as they lead the new church in a time of opposition and personal threats (Matthew 6:25–34).

Stress has been a part of the human life since the fall of this world, and we all know the negative effects of stress. Yet, seasons of stress are a guarantee. Most of us also know that for teenagers, stress can be exaggerated and come from seemingly bizarre sources. For the teen with ADHD, stress is even more magnified.

Some of our most challenging teenage parenting moments were during periods of elevated stress. In Wesley's case, high stress levels were almost always accompanied by behavioral infractions and out-bursts of anger. Oftentimes we would see these first before becoming aware of the obvious stress in his life we somehow missed. Other times, we were unable to positively identify the source. No matter the cause, parents must be able to manage their teen during times of stress while dealing with their own stress, often from the same source. I found the following to be effective tools to carry in my Handy-Dandy Teenage Tool Bag:

SCOUTS, BE ALERT—When an obvious stress has taken place in the life of your teen, a simple heads-up can make all the differ-ence. As you brace yourself for impact, also notify your child's teachers and school faculty of the recent event(s) and of possible upcoming behavior challenges.

TALK TIME—Allow your teen the opportunity to vent. Some per-sonalities are talkers and will debrief themselves with someone they feel comfortable talking to. Do everything in your power to be the listener they feel comfortable with. No matter how incon-venient the time, STOP—LOOK—and LISTEN when your child initiates a venting session. Don't try to solve every problem at that very moment with interruptions of advice (one of my biggest challenges). This can cause the teen to become defensive. JUST LISTEN. Only after your teen has vented completely will you be able to offer BRIEF words of parental guidance. If your child is one that is less open about their feelings or your normally talkative teen has suddenly bottled up, seize the best moment and ask your child about their feelings. I found that when Wesley was alone and quiet was the best time for this. Sometimes a simple comment with a question was all it took. No matter if your teen initiates talking or you do, or even if he/she refuses to talk at all, always end with words of encouragement.

ALLOW APPROPRIATE OUTLETS—The most obvious by-products of stress are negative energy and emotion. The teen with ADHD is no exception to the rule and is more likely an exaggeration to the rule. Negative emotions must be processed and the energy released. If appropriate outlets are not allowed, negative energy may be released in inappropriate and destructive ways, causing increased stress and a spinning negative cycle. Talking about the stress, journaling, or drawing, playing video games or listening to music (yes, loud) are excellent ways to process negative emotion as these activate both hemispheres of the brain. However, negative energy may still remain. At times, your teenager may need to release negative energy before he/she is able to process negative emotion. Activities your child enjoys can make for very good outlets.

During Wesley's teen years, he was able to release negative energy by doing projects or activities (physically active) with his friends and cousin. We allowed these outlets and accommodated them as quickly and as much as possible. Sometimes, Wes required more immediate and intense outlets and was allowed to strike unbreakable objects in his room or a fence post outside with a plastic bat. Find whatever activities and outlets you can to allow your child opportunity to process negative emotion and release negative energy.

REMEMBER MEDICATION—There is not a more crucial time for medication than when your teen is experiencing stress. Yet, it is during this time that medication is most often neglected. It is common for teens and their parents to already be less compliant with medication and medicating during life's smooth runs. As a result, everyone is out of habit when stress ensues. There were many times it seemed to take us hours, if not days, to remember to medicate. But with every passing year we got better and better.

Ignore/Acknowledge

THERE WERE TIMES that I felt overwhelmed by all the scientific, tactical, and practical information I had either sought out for myself or was given by well-meaning "opinionists." Perhaps you have had the same experience or are feeling overwhelmed right now as you read.

I sympathize.

I thank God for so many things He has taught me. And Ignore/Acknowledge is no exception. It is one of the most rewarding of simplicity skills. It was not only helpful during Wesley's young years, but also up to the day he packed his room and moved into his own place. Right up to the shutting of the door.

Ignore/Acknowledge is a practical, minute-by-minute, hour-by-hour survival tool that combines Choosing Your Battles and Removing the Audience on a smaller scale. It is basically the practice of ignoring negative behavior and acknowledging positive behavior. Now, don't misunderstand me. As one should do when choosing battles, a parent must acknowledge and address some negative behavior. But acknowledging negative behavior that is not worthy of intervention is a waste of precious energy and, in my experience, only makes matters worse.

Wesley's need to move and create noise was the most common of this type of negative behavior. Many times, the duration of the exhibited behavior was shortened when I simply acted as though I noticed nothing of what he was doing. And as soon as he stopped, I would try to acknowledge his presence. For example, when Wes incessantly banged his fork on his plate, tapped his feet on the floor, or moved his chair back and forth at the dinner table, it behooved us all to ignore him. Most of the time this type of behavior was purposeful, our reaction meant purely for Wes's entertainment. If we acknowledged his behavior or showed any sign of irritation, he would only intensify what he was doing and a battle would ensue. Family dinner would be ruined with Wes angry, eating in his room, and the rest of the family deflated, eating at the table. But if his behavior was successfully ignored, or at least got very little attention, Wesley usually discontinued what he was doing in a matter of minutes.

There were times when Wes would exhibit negative behavior unconsciously and in similar or even identical manners as purposeful negative behavior. This usually happened when he was nervous. During these times, I found it appropriate to gently make Wesley aware of what he was doing. A simple hand placed on the shoulder, arm, hand, or leg, or a gentle reminding whisper was usually all it took. It was during moments like these that Wes did NOT want to bring attention to himself and welcomed the help.

I realize this technique takes practice and may come easier to some than others. But I guarantee IT WORKS and that it is worth the initial effort it may take to make it a habit for simplifying day-to-day life. Once you have developed the skill to Ignore/Acknowledge, you can then help to train others in the family to do the same.

Physical Affection

THE GOSPELS OF the Bible record just a few of the many miracles Jesus performed every day during His three-year ministry. One can only imagine the true number of people the Lord blessed with physical and spiritual healing, and therefore, the true number of people He literally touched.

In most of the miracles where Jesus was physically present, it is also recorded that He physically touched. This was not necessary for the miracle to be performed. All the Lord had to do was speak the words and it was so. Yet, He added the special blessing of touch each time (Matthew 8:1–15; 9:18–29; 15:21–28; 17:5–7).

God made the world to go around by creating human individuality and personality differences. Some individuals are extroverted, outgoing, and interact more physically with others. Yet some personalities are introverted, quiet, and interact less physically with others. And some are somewhere in between. Then, there are folks we know who are just simply from another planet. But no matter a person's personality, age, or what planet they come from, human touch is a necessary component of complete personal wellness. It is a God-given need. Do not hesitate to show your child affection through the amazing power of touch. From a brief pat on the shoulder to a full-blown hug with a kiss, there are many appropriate ways to show physical affection to a child. Even teenagers will tolerate and benefit from these displays of affection, despite their "I'm too cool and too old" stances and verbal expressions of disgust. Be sure to take time for this.

I was an energetic and busy mom with projects and activities both with and without the children. As a result, I had a tendency to be in a bit of a rush at times. Thankfully, through the wisdom of others, God taught me to STOP—RECIPROCATE—WAIT.

- STOP whatever it is you are doing when your child initiates physical affection.
- RECIPROCATE this affection.
- WAIT for the child to break contact.

This simple guideline became a way of life for me that resulted in great benefits.

I believe touch to be a vital part of loving and raising any child and to be ten times more powerful for the child with ADHD.

Life with Wesley had not ever been boring and only became

more and more interesting with each passing year of adventures. By the end of his fifteenth year, I knew we had only begun to experience the increasing intensity of life lessons to come. But I also knew with 100 percent certainty that Wesley was going to make it. God had been clear about this.

He reminded me daily, "Wes just needs time and repetition. He is going to make it. I'm going to make sure of it. And you, Mom, need me more than ever. Come to me."

Oh, how right He was!

4

Ages 16-19

"What a handsome young man . . . He didn't . . . Oh dear!"

IT WAS A cold December night.

Jami was nestled all snug in her bed The covers pulled up to her little blond head.

And Kevin in his undershorts and I in my gown Were taking a winter's nap and had just settled down. (So it seemed.)

When at the front door there arose such a clatter.

It was a strong knock.

It was Penny!

It was 4:00 in the morning.

Wes was sleeping over at her house.

This did not look good!

"I have been trying to call you guys all night," Penny said as she stepped inside.

"Oh, Penny, I'm sorry. We have the phones off." (Something we did when receiving incessant phone calls from intoxicated family members.) "What is going on?" I replied.

"I can't find the boys!"

Penny went on to explain that she began looking for Wesley and her son, Colin, at about midnight when they did not return home as expected. She advised us that earlier in the evening the boys were in town with their friends Brandon and Josh and had reportedly gone to the home of some people that Brandon knew. Penny knew the location of the home and had driven there to look for the boys.

"I know they're there but THAT WOMAN won't let me in to look for them or send them out. The woman says that Josh had been drinking and took off walking and that the boys went to look for him," Penny said. "I think they are in the house, and she's hiding them."

Immediately visions of patients who had succumbed to hypothermia flashed through my mind. I envisioned the boys intoxicated and outside without proper clothing.

The unanimous decision to involve law enforcement and go back to the home was made quickly. Daelin stayed at our home with Jami while Penny and Kevin and I headed back to town.

I uttered the first of several private prayers as the helights shined the way through the dark, empty streets. We arrived in the area of the suspected house and met with the responding police officer who Kevin knew and I was familiar with. (Being acquainted with police officers was a perk of our jobs.) He was apprised of the situation, and then went to the house. Without hesitation, the woman let him in, and within minutes, he brought out with him both Wes and Colin. The officer told us that he found one boy under a bed and the other in a closet, hiding. The woman claimed that she did not know the boys were there. The boys were mildly intoxicated, inappropriately relaxed about their situation, and in a WHOLE LOT OF TROUBLE. We were greatly relieved, but we were also angry about the fact that nothing could be done concerning the adult who helped our juvenile children hide in her home. We thanked the officer for his assistance, and he drove off to begin his search for Josh. Josh was later found safe.

Brandon, the oldest of the boys, was in the woman's home the entire time and had hidden his truck from view. On this night, Kevin and I red-flagged Brandon and regarded him with high suspicion from then on.

Obviously, the boys had agreed to the activities of the evening. We hoped this first was the last of their episodes with alcohol. But Kevin and I knew that for Wesley, it probably wasn't. His need for more repetition in order to learn had us anticipating the next adventure.

And the boy did not deprive us of it.

Only a short time later, Wes, Colin, and my nephew Chris had another drink fest while adults were sleeping. Brandon had snuck over in the night and supplied the alcohol. They were caught. But we were worried. Where was this going? Was this normal, innocent curiosity? Or were we merely seeing the preview to the blockbuster.

Wesley was no stranger to the dark side of alcohol and alcoholism as well as drug dependency. He had heard his grandmother talk of the struggles of his uncles (my brothers) when young. And by the time he was sixteen, he saw it firsthand.

My mother had become ill with multiple myeloma. During the year of her illness, my husband was involved in a car accident that killed a woman. The accident was not his fault but difficult for him nonetheless. Physically, only his leg was broken. But emotionally, much more was at stake. It was during this year, while my mother was in hospitals and my husband was injured that my brothers and their substance abuse began to affect my life and the lives of my family. At the time of my mother's death, my father had been dead for less than four years. Suddenly my brothers sought after me as parent/big sister and began taxing my patience the way they had my parents for years. They took turns needing "a place to stay for a while," and we opened our home to them. As a result, Wesley witnessed their behavior when drinking and using and was audience to the tough love I had to use to survive.

Due to the high level of stress, setting boundaries, enforcing deadlines, and practicing a no-tolerance policy came much easier for me than it might have otherwise. The reality was that I, my home, and family could take no more. Five days after I had kicked one brother out of my home for infractions, the other brother moved in. As it was with the first, he had nowhere else to go and was sure he could abide by the rules of the home. He even felt he could be of assistance to us. For the first week, he followed through. But by the second week, he could maintain no longer. The next day, this brother was escorted to the bus station and put on a bus to catch a train.

He caught the train.

Sometime later, the first brother was escorted to an airport to catch a plane.

He caught the plane.

Both brothers were offered the opportunity to walk into a rehabilitation facility of their choice, paid in full. The monies would come out of their portion of the estate of our parents, fronted to the facility by me. They both took advantage of the opportunity. The trains and planes took them to these facilities. Praise God, for it was He that made the timing of loss to be good for gain. My brothers checked themselves into rehabilitation. But their stories are each another book.

I praise God for the life lessons my children were able to see. I believe God used these very negative experiences in our home to teach me tough love and to head Wesley off at the pass. After these experiences with his uncles and his own teen drinking misadventures, Wes's curiosity and need to experiment with alcohol while living at home became less.

The following are what I found to be the most impending teenage issues and God's guidance concerning them:

Teens and Alcohol/Drugs

MOST PARENTS UNDERSTAND the dangerous and debilitating threat that alcohol and drugs are to our children. The fact that the teenager with ADHD has an even greater potential for substance abuse takes this parental scare off the chart, not to mention the predisposed conditions of our children due to inherited and learned behavioral traits.

There are so many aspects of our teens' lives that we are unable to control. And every passing year leaves us with less and less. This is part of the maturing process, whether we like it or not. And in my experience, the harder a parent tries to control their teenager, the less control they have. The BACKFIRE is unmistakable and is always detrimental.

At the time of writing this book, a growing population of depressed and addicted young people has been developing for several decades in the United States.

Much information exists and opinions abound that address the possible reasons for this.

For me, the bottom line was that I was living and raising my children in a fallen world—an imperfect world. I could not expect perfection of myself and how I raised the children. I could not expect perfection of my husband and how he dealt with the children. And I certainly could not expect perfection of the children. All I could do was do the best I could to follow God's guidance and leave the rest up to Him.

God had proven to me that He could be trusted. That He would always guide me. I just had to listen. God was in control. I wasn't, and neither was Satan. Some of the influence of alcohol and drugs in Wesley's life was out of my control. But it was not out of God's control. It was God's time and not my time that my son's life was subject to. And God's time was perfect.

That being said, parents MUST be proactive. For me, this meant communicating. I had to share with Wes my experiences and therefore expectations of anyone living in our home concerning alcohol and drug use. And then, I had to enforce my expectations.

Alcohol and drug use is absolutely a battle to choose. Yet, along with sex, this battle is one of the most challenging. It usually comes at a time when we, as parents, are already struggling with the balance between letting go and holding on. We choose the alcohol/drug battle. We deem it important. But, we are also being forced to let go. And for some parents, the teen years have worn them down so far they feel no other alternative but to give up, to let go entirely.

STOP!

God NEVER GIVES UP on us. We must NEVER GIVE UP on our children. My parents were praying for my brothers and me and offered guidance and advice up to the day they died. They refused to give up. Throughout the years, we witnessed the ongoing miracles their prayers continued to bring and the influence their wise words continued to have on us. Most important, however, was the example of how they lived their lives. This had the most impact. Both the things they did well and the mistakes they made, God made to be of good influence.

The following are what God convinced me to be of most importance when dealing with my teenager and alcohol and drugs:

PRAY—As it should be in all aspects of our lives, prayer must be the first thing we do concerning any situation.

This did not come naturally for me. The act of actually presenting a matter to God usually was the second or third thing I did. For years, I battered myself about this, until one day when the Lord made me realize that what I did first was instinctively respond to whatever needed my attention. And HE was speaking to me through my instincts. I was listening to the voice of God! It wasn't that I was SO SMART. It was that GOD was PERFECTLY WISE. Yet, I must admit that the battle of alcohol and drugs was one of several that sent me to my knees quickly. It was during these times of uncertainty and lack of control that God reminded me of how much I needed Him.

When we pray for guidance concerning our children, our instincts, emotions, and thought processes are influenced by God. If we allow Him to control these, then the outcome is also His. Whew, what a relief!

I thank the Lord for challenges so great that I had no other choice but to turn to Him. These taught me to better hear the Lord's voice, even when I was strutting around, thinking I had it all figured out. I didn't. But God did. Once again, pray for your children without ceasing.

INFORMATION, LOCATION, DURATION—In our home, Kevin was the driven parent. He needed and wanted information in as much detail as possible. Kevin insisted on knowing Wesley's location. And he required and enforced duration. Kevin helped me to learn the importance of knowing what your child is doing and whom he is with, where your child is and how long your child plans to be at a given location, as well as his expected time back at home. I playfully called it, "God Is Watching." But Wes knew it was not a joke. It was a safety issue of great importance. As seasoned paramedics, Kevin and I had repetitively seen the sad outcome of the teen that had made a bad choice. Of course, some accidents were truly accidents. No parent intends for their child to get hurt. But a pattern of obvious misguidance and lack of parenting in many of these ill-fated youth could not be denied.

I'm sure Wesley and his friends got tired of us sharing our horror stories about the calls we had been on. And, I'm sure Wes took a lot of grief from his friends concerning his parents. Yet, "God Is Watching" had a nifty side effect. Wes was a little paranoid. The fact that on occasion we would randomly show up to check on him and anyone with him deterred them all from making some bad judgment calls. Kevin was especially good at this and was usually the one who caught Wesley in the act of making a poor decision. Of course, we did not always feel it necessary to check on Wes. It was also important that he be allowed the opportunity to be trusted. Yet, when the boy wanted to go camping with several other teenage boys and without adult supervision, our Parent Alert Alarms sounded.

Let the common sense that God has given you be your guide. Be smart!

Also, don't forget to take advantage of modern technology. Most teenagers want anything that is considered popular to have. And modern technology is usually at the top of the list. Anything that assists a parent in communicating with and tracking their child is very useful. For us, the cell phone was this tool. For Wesley, it was "cool," "awesome," and "bad" to have a cell phone for obvious teenage reasons. But for Kevin and me, it was all about safety.

I encourage every parent of any teen to insist on Information, Location, and Duration.

BE A FUN PARENT—Don't let your parenting become solely the job of dealing with issues, disciplining, and problem solving. Teenagers are FUN. And the teen with ADHD has been practicing how to have fun for years. Wesley never ran out of ideas and energy when it came to having fun. He was creative, spontaneous, and upbeat and not ever lacking for friends. Our home was constantly bustling with children of all ages and whatever it was they were doing, with Wes leading the pack. If your child loves to keep moving and engaged in stimulating activities with his/her friends, don't be a dud! JOIN THEM! You can take extra overtime hours at work next time. The chores can wait. The TV program is not that good. (You can watch it later.) STOP what you're doing, GET UP off the couch, and GET GOING. Let all your adult worries go for a while and PLAY. Whatever activity your child finds enjoyable, do it with him/her. Even better, you be the one to plan it. Make being with the family super teenage friendly.

Also if your child seems to need them, accommodate as many guests as you can.

On paper I had two children. But no one watching us on a day-to-day basis would have believed it. Outings, trips, special occasions, and even daily events such as shopping and the evening meal usually included more than one each of Wes's and Jami's friends, in addition to their inseparable cousins.

Take initiative and make hanging out with the family to be where your child and his/her friends want to be. Yes, it takes energy and resources to do this. But the nights that I crawled into bed or into a sleeping bag exhausted and broke because I had had so much fun with the children were the best nights of my life. It was a wonderful feeling to fall asleep, knowing that all of those kids would rather be with me than somewhere else.

I thank God for a life full of such nights. Let God fill your life with fun times with your children so that they are less likely to find their fun somewhere else.

Teens and Work/School Balance

KEVIN AND I anticipated Wesley becoming of age to get a job for a couple of years before he actually could. The same was true with how we felt about him being able to drive on his own. By the time Wes turned sixteen and became eligible and legal to do both of these things, Kevin and I were ready for a break. Each year, Wesley's teenage needs were more expensive and time-consuming than the year before. And as mentioned previously, we did not ever have just one teen. No matter where or what we were doing, we came in droves.

Due to the financial demands of teens, it is easy for parents to want, hope, or even expect their child to be able to take most of the load off of them once their teenager is able to secure employment. Or, some parents may find that their child would prefer to work rather than do anything else, like go to school. Still, other parents may feel utter hopelessness because their teenager seems to have no desire to work at all.

Through my experience with my child with ADHD, God showed me the single most important thing to remember concerning the above issues:

AVOID OVERWHELMING—Be careful not to overwhelm your teen with the added responsibility of working in addition to schooling. It helped me to keep in mind that these early years of employment were primarily meant for learning experiences. They were not meant for financial security and independence. It was important to me that schooling was PRIORITY ONE and that this was clear to everyone.

Of course, every parent is governed differently depending on a household's financial status. If at all possible, avoid overwhelming your child with the expectation that you will depend on his income as part of the household budget. Yes, your teen is now old enough to begin doing as much as he can to pay for his own extra expenses, thus assisting financially in the home. This alone may be very helpful. But the teenager with ADHD can be easily overwhelmed when he feels pressured to take on more than he is capable of processing. When this happens, attitudes become negative. Thus, the opportunity for a positive learning experience turns into a negative episode before it can even get off the ground.

Be easy on yourself. The breaking point for any teen changes from day to day. Use common sense and your own judgment to guide you. Remember from earlier in this book, "the one sure thing is change." Be sure. The day you become convinced that your own offspring has no work ethic at all will be the day before he/she turns around and surprises you.

Teens and Medication

AS WESLEY GREW from a child to a young man, my approach to medication concerning him had to grow and change as well. It was during this age period that I felt he should be allowed more independence and the opportunity to rely on his own judgment about his medication. In so doing, I also had to embrace any negative repercussions that resulted as Wes experimented with his increased freedom. As had been the case with many rearing decisions concerning Wesley, I received some opposing opinion on the matter from well-meaning family and friends. But the idea burned strong in my gut, the place where God communicated best with me, and that's all I needed. I knew it would not be easy, but I also trusted God. He had not ever and would not ever lead me astray. If I was wrong, He would show me and use the experience in a positive way. He always did. By this time, I KNEW this.

As one might imagine, Wes's first instinct was to decide not to take a scheduled dose of his medication, justified by one reason or another. As had been the case for many years, Kevin and I found ourselves assisting Wesley in recognizing the correlation between behavior problems and noncompliance with medication and/or poor eating habits. Even though these experiences were sometimes intense and difficult, the opportunity to learn from them was invaluable. And he did learn, although it took some repetition. But reality life lessons of any kind were most productive for Wes. And during his teens, they also provided opportunities to remind him of the rank of household members. I often said to Wes, "You are the prince. But I am the QUEEN."

For example, on three separate occasions during Wesley's mid-teen years, his poor judgment resulted in a repeated reality life lesson.

It was and will always be my strong belief that respect is an earned honor. And by goodness, I had earned respect, deserved it, and would have it! So when Wes was unable to restrain himself from disrespecting me while en route to whatever destination we were headed, he was warned of his impending removal from the vehicle should he verbally abuse me again. On these three specific occasions, Wes's downward path to being on foot was inevitable. Once while on the way to get movies, about one mile from our destination, he walked. Once while on the way to see a movie, about one mile from our destination, he walked. (Is anyone seeing a pattern here?) And once while on the way to a birthday party at a park, about three miles from our destination, he walked. I never worried about the boy alone on foot. I knew he was just as angry as I was and therefore just as capable of fending off anyone who tried to mess with him. He always showed up to the destination, nose out of joint but mouth SHUT.

The Queen had spoken.

Granted, there were times we insisted Wesley take his medication. But the reality I wished for him to learn about independence was that the world would always be able to deal with him. But it was he who must learn to deal with himself in the world. And the reality I wished to reiterate to Wes was that medication was a tool available to him to assist him in using capabilities he already had. Like many things in independent life, medication was a choice.

The summer that followed graduation, Wesley continued working at his first job and remained there a year. This was another miracle from God. The job was boring, repetitive, and uninteresting. As we had learned, these were the three worst enemies of ADHD.

The rules set up for Wes about living at home after graduating from high school was that his room and board were free as long as he was schooling. If he chose not to school, then he must pay room and board. When Wesley was nineteen years old, the independence I had been encouraging took its first steps and he moved out of the house. He and his childhood buddy Daelin split the rent on a lot of land a stone's throw away. Wes's dad, Kelly, cosigned on a small loan for Wes so he could buy the trailer home that was on the lot. Once again, God had worked everything out. The realization that Kevin and I were unable to handle any more stressors made saying no to a cosign an easy decision. As a result, Wesley asked Kelly for help. And it was certainly Kelly's turn. PERFECT.

For the first year, Wes did very well. He landed a good job and managed his money well enough that we heard nothing of financial dilemmas. But bad luck was soon to strike.

5

Ages 20-23

"Man-Child . . . It's a jungle out there!"

WES AND DAELIN did well as roommates, sharing not only expenses but the duties of the home. To my surprise and joy, the same young man whose room in my home was a hazardous materials area, had much higher expectations of neatness and cleanliness in the living area of his own home. And Daelin loved to cook. So Wes cleaned and Daelin cooked.

I was proud of the boys. They were good to take in a friend in need whenever possible. And even though their home was indeed a bachelor pad, complete with certain underage privileges, they set and enforced other important boundaries. I praised God when I learned that my son had followed through with his word and kicked a roommate out of his home who insisted on using drugs. It was a difficult thing to do as the roommate was an old friend. Wesley's heart was big with compassion and a will to help others. So, I was happy to see that he was able to administer tough love at such a young age.

Yet, life's bumps in the road can always be counted on.

On a summer day during Wes's twentieth year, while attempting to load his ATV in the back of his truck, one of the ramps slipped and the four-wheeler rocked off balance. In order to avoid being crushed under the ATV, Wesley sprang away from the vehicle and landed in a bad position on his foot, fracturing several bones in it. After seeing the orthopedic physician and learning of his inability to use his foot for many weeks, Wes's employer felt he had no other choice than to let him go. Before the bad week could come to a close, Wesley's girlfriend broke up with him as well.

On a day shortly after, Wes said to me, "Man, I sound like a country song!"

His humor was obviously intact. But, the impact of the events caused Wes to realize his need for change. A few months after enjoying employment as a cook at Chilies Restaurant, Wesley rallied together with a group of new friends and moved to Phoenix to work for Chilies there and enjoy a change of scenery. I supported the idea in spite of its spontaneity and slightly poor planning. I knew God was working something out and that all was for a reason.

Wesley quickly landed a job with Chilies Restaurant and, just as quickly, began living a swinging single's lifestyle. He liked his work but had trouble getting enough hours. Therefore, lessons of money constraints also came quickly.

Wes's choice to move away from home and work instead of live at home and school was exactly that: a choice. And it was important that I allow reality to play its part. Wesley may not have been enrolled in an institute of learning, but he was enrolled in the school of real life. Allowing reality to play its part was not easy and was not always done perfectly. But praise God for giving me the strength to do it better than I would have on my own.

I believe mothers are instilled with an inherent nature to protect. All creation exemplifies this. Animal mothers have been known to not only kill but to give their own lives in order to protect their young. The species must survive.

Human mothers are no different. They, too, have an instinct to protect their young at all cost. Yet, unlike animals, the outcome has many variables and impacts their offspring differently. Situations are sometimes convoluted and without clear indications of right and wrong.

The saying, "There is no right or wrong, only opinion," has been seen by some as a cop-out for living a moral life. But in many other instances, it bears much truth.

The bottom line for me was that once I felt convinced I SHOULD intervene on my son's behalf and interfere with reality, it was not up for discussion.

THE SPECIES MUST SURVIVE!

Likewise, when I decided to allow Wes to experience reality-life lessons, I dug my heels in, wrapped the rope around my hip, and stood my ground.

THE COLT MUST BE TRAINED!

Once again, the one sure thing is change. And just when I thought my son would do nothing but live a life of mostly irresponsibility, God shook it up.

As one might expect, Wesley's inexperience and free-fun lifestyle made for financial shortcomings. We were aware of his struggles because he had asked us for help and we had told him we were unable. Wes had expressed that he was behind on his vehicle payments and feared his truck may be repossessed.

One morning I received a distressed call from Wesley. "Mom, my truck is gone!" he exclaimed. "What do I do?"

"Well, honey, did it get repossessed?" I asked in a calm voice.

"I don't think so. I think it got stolen, right here at the apartments last night."

"We need to find out for sure."

Upon further investigation, we discovered that it had not been repossessed and immediately reported it stolen.

Several days later Wesley called again. "Mom, they found my truck just south of the border in Mexico. It was totaled."

This time, God had intervened. Instead of losing his truck due to repossession and marring his already-tattered credit, Wes was able to make an insurance claim on the stolen vehicle and reinvest in a more economical car. And his parents were spared the tension of allowing reality to play its part. God was amazing and did this on more than one occasion.

When God intervenes, the last word is spoken.

Of course, insurance claims and automobile purchases take time. Thankfully, Wes lived near his work and other shopping and was able to use a bicycle while waiting.

After the insurance claim was processed and Wesley had his money, we made a trip to visit, bring him some other belongings, and allow Kevin to shop with Wes for another vehicle. It was on this trip that I saw again the power of prayer and realized God had succeeded in stirring my son's heart.

On the second evening of our visit, we filed into our van and headed for a nearby restaurant for dinner. The van was full as we had additional passengers and Wes and I ended up sitting in the far back seat together. We chatted about cell phones, the weather, and his work as a cook.

As we ventured in the conversation of work, Wes said, "Mom, I really like cooking. I think I'd like to go to culinary school."

With a sudden leap in my heart and without hesitation, I said, "Wes, that's a great idea!"

"Yeah, I've been talking to people here and there are several really good culinary schools in this area."

"I've heard that too. You can absolutely go to school. We'll look into it."

How, where, or when did not matter to me. My son wanted to further his education and better himself! This I would support, and I would have words with anyone who said I shouldn't.

And they did.

Raising a challenging child with overly cautious, intense-thinking family members had taught me well when to engage in a debate and how, and when not to. I learned how to express and justify my instinctive decisions, to stand firm on them, and fend off any unwelcome advances that tried to deny me the right to act on them. Supporting Wesley's desire to go to culinary school was my most challenging standoff. Because it involved a significant financial commitment, I claimed my right of financial equality and independence and applied for financial aid on my own. The aid was granted. I also applied for a small credit card for Wes to use while in school, as he would only be working part time. The card was granted.

Sometime before this, I had researched the schools in the Phoenix area and found the Arizona Culinary Institute (ACI) in Scottsdale to be the most appealing for several reasons. It was a technical school, offering a certificate in Culinary Arts and Restaurant Management. The training lasted just under a year and could be applied toward a college degree. The cost was comparative. But what sold me the most was the thrilling telephone call I received from Wesley after touring the school.

"Mom . . . oh, Mom . . . the school is awesome . . . The kitchens are huge and so amazing . . . You should see all the ovens and pots and appliances . . . They have these huge mixers and big walk-in coolers and freezer . . . And they have a restaurant where the students take turns serving and cooking . . . The students have to make up the menu themselves . . . But that's toward the end of the training . . . Oh, Mom . . . the instructors are so cool . . . I like this one chef . . . He's big, has tattoos and smokes and looks a biker, and he and I really hit off . . . They were all really great . . . They seem to really want me to get in . . . Do you think I'll get in?" Wes rattled with an enthusiasm I had not heard since he was a young boy.

"I don't see why not. I'll get back online and pay the fee to secure you a spot for class starting in August while we wait for the financial aid to come through," I said with confidence.

I had studied the Web site several times and was aware that there were still openings and had noticed that a spot could be reserved. It was done immediately and looked to be good. But before I could re-cover the energy it took to defend my decision to send Wes to school, ACI denied him a position in August. The school said that we had to have the financial aid come through by an earlier deadline and had missed it by three days.

My motherly blood BOILED! This information was not clear on the Web site. Wes was geared and ready and also believed he would

TAKE YOUR PILLS AND GO TO YOUR ROOM

start school soon. I begged and pleaded with the coordinator. I told him of the lack of clarity on the matter. But he stood firm. Wes would have to wait for the next class that began six weeks later.

"Six weeks!"

I informed the coordinator that getting Wesley into the school as soon as possible was imperative and that I feared we would lose him in six weeks. Wes was ON FIRE now! But that fire would go out.

The coordinator seemed unmoved.

My heart told me that if I could get Wes in now, he would finish. God was speaking. Yet, I couldn't understand. If this was what God wanted, why could I not convince the coordinator to make an exception?

My phone call to Wes was one of defeat, sorrow, and much apology for the disappointment. My voice cracked with emotion. None of these were common. And just as my blood had boiled for my son, Wes's blood boiled for me. He told me nothing of what he was going to do. But what he did, God used.

Twenty-four hours later, Wesley called. "Hey, Mom, I just want to let you know that I just got off the phone with the coordinator at ACI, and I lined some things out. I was respectful, but I told him of my disappointment in the school and the way they handled our attempt to jump through all the hoops and meet deadlines that were not clearly made known to us," he said self-assuredly. "I told him that I really wanted to attend their school and that my mother had beat herself into the ground trying to get me in and that I was terribly disappointed. I was careful not to shoot myself in the foot, but I really wanted them to understand how discouraging this was."

The voice on the phone sounded like that of a businessman, rather than that of the tattooed and pierced man child I was accustomed to. I told Wes that I was proud of him taking a stance and that he had done a good job. The conversation ended with a settling into how we would get in later. It was a Friday. I could not have ever anticipated what happened the following Monday.

The phone rang.

"Hello."

"Mrs. Jones," a man's voice said.

"Yes."

"This is the coordinator at ACI. I received a phone call from your son, Wesley, last week. And well . . . I got a butt chewing, but let me just say that I couldn't get you and your son off of my mind," the man informed me. "So much so, that I called my coworker in the finance department here at the school and we discussed the matter. We've decided to do something we've not ever done. We're going to bend the rules a bit and let Wes begin schooling with the students in August."

My heart leapt with joy. I thanked him again and again. And when I hung up the phone, I thanked and praised God.

Wes was elated upon hearing the news and took over all correspondence and planning and began meeting appointments with the school to prepare for class to begin. I washed my hands of my duties. It was now his responsibility to make it all work. I had done my part.

For the next two months, I received regular phone calls from Wesley. Most calls were those of excitement and joy and thanks. Occasionally, Wes would talk of difficult academic assignments, talk of how a student had dropped out, and express self-doubt. During the school's weeks of intense academics, including terminology, chemistry, and mathematics, it also included daily hands-on lessons in the kitchen. The balance was perfect for my son, but nothing to shake a stick at. There were times I had to encourage Wes and remind him of the gratification to come. But most of the time, he needed no real support. And when the grades started coming in and Wesley was able to see the fruits of his labor, it was all he needed.

I remember the phone call I received after he had gotten the results back from the final test of the first section.

"Mom, I got a B on my test! I got a B! I'm going to get an A on the next one," he reported happily.

"*That's* what I'm talkin' about!" I said proudly. "I knew you could do it. I wasn't even worried."

And it was the truth.

I believe that when God works a miracle, worrying about details afterword (although common human nature) is a bit disrespectful.

Sometime after the holidays, I received an especially excited phone call from Wesley.

"You'll never guess what I might get to do!" he exclaimed. "The TV show *Dinner Impossible* has decided to film an episode here in Phoenix and is going to use some of the students from ACI in the show. I'm going to interview with the show's audition people and see if they pick me to be on the show," he said decidedly and with excitement.

"Son, that's incredible! What an amazing opportunity," I said with equal excitement.

And about a week later, Wes informed us that he and his roommate both had been selected to be two of the five students that would be in the show.

The weeks that followed we received regular updates. Wes and his fellow students had met Chef Robert and although appropriately intimidated by the reality star, they found him to be friendly and full of fun when off camera. Wes told us of the hours of footage recorded for what would only be an hour show, including commercials. He suspected he was going to be singled out as the bad apple but said he didn't care. When the show aired, Wesley's family and friends accounted for what must have been half of his community's viewers. The fun that the students had filming came across on screen. And as it turned out, Wes was not depicted as the bad apple. Mamma liked that.

Chef Robert would not have wanted for me to have WORDS with him.

The remainder of Wes's training went by quickly and smoothly and when it was over, he proudly completed all requirements and tests with an 88 percent average.

God can do ANYTHING.

In April, between completing training and graduation from ACI, Wes and his roommate, Andrew, were able to practice all they had learned.

Jami was turning twelve. Sometime before that, she was convicted by the Lord to dedicate her life to Him and planned to be baptized on her birthday. The day fell on a Sabbath.

Of course, baptisms are big deals by themselves. So it went without saying that a baptism on a birthday required a major celebration.

Upon informing Wes of the upcoming event so that he could plan to attend, I also told him of my plans to have it catered. He immediately told me of how he would like to cater the event and scolded me for not asking him first.

"I can do it, Mom. I'll see if Andrew can come and help me. And with the help of the family in the kitchen, we can do this!"

"That sounds great! Let me know as soon as you can if you and Andrew get the time off."

After this, I remained on the phone for quite some time as Wes excitedly talked about ideas for dishes, sides, and desserts, and whether he should serve the dinner plated or buffet-style.

A short time later, Wesley confirmed his commitment and informed us that he and Andrew would arrive the night before the event and that it would be a plated dinner. We gave him a head count (the estimated attendance at church that day), and he later gave us a menu and an impressive grocery list.

Jami continued her studies with Pastor Herra, the pastor of her upbringing who baptized Wes, their Aunt Cindy and Jami's best friend, Katie in the pond a few years before. I took care of the announcements and arrangements at church. Kevin and I went on a shopping extravaganza and checked off all items on the grocery list. With the donation of additional pots and pans, utensils, and kitchen appliances, the church kitchen was equipped and ready. And as the sun set the evening before bringing in the Sabbath, the all-purpose room off the kitchen was set with clothed tables and centerpieces.

The next morning was an early one. Under the direction of Wes, the entire family, including Penny, Cindy, Chris and his girlfriend, Taree,carried out assignments in the kitchen. The menu included:

- Aunt Cindy's Rolls
- Salad
- Split Pea Soup
- Eggplant Parmesan
- Vegetarian-Stuffed Bell Peppers
- Gourmet Macaroni and Cheese
- Gourmet Mashed Potatoes
- Steamed Vegetables
- Layered Chocolate Mousse Pudding and Fruit
- Angel Eggs (a Wes original, made of custard shaped in egg molds to look like Deviled Eggs, served as dessert.)

Andrew was in charge of sauces and soups and Cindy of rolls, each their specialties. Kevin and I assisted Wes with entrées, salad, and dessert, his burden of choice. And everyone helped everywhere. Jami, Katie, and Sarah helped in the kitchen until time to get dressed and ready for church. I was also in charge of the music and worship leading for the church service that morning and removed myself from the kitchen sometime before to get ready with the girls.

Just before church began, I stood with my daughter and gazed upon her reflection in the mirror. Her aqua eyes and slightly turned up nose accented her beautiful face, topped with a head of golden hair and sparkling head band. The pink of her flowing, baptism Sabbath outfit radiated the flush of her pink skin. I looked on her proudly, but not for this obvious outside beauty. It was the beauty on the inside that God had made in her that was most impressive. Yes, I was a proud mom. But it was God who deserved all the glory for the busy, happy rattling in the kitchen and the glow of His child in the mirror.

The church pews were full as the service began and the Holy Spirit took over, just the way He should. In music and with praises to God, Jami was submerged under the water. As the pastor lifted her from the water, memories of my own baptism ignited a recommitment to the Lord in my heart.

Praise God!

When the service was over, we all returned to the kitchen as the guests took their seats and filled the tables. Dinner was blessed and the business of plating and serving began. I marveled at how particular my son was about the presentation of the plates as he personally and precisely filled each one.

The food was indeed beautiful.

It took a dozen people and about forty-five minutes to serve all the guests. But no one complained and all seemed to enjoy. When everyone had opportunity for seconds and dessert and the celebration cake was served, Wes and Andrew were asked to come out of the kitchen to be recognized. With loud applause and wearing their smudged chef coats, they took a gracious bow.

How good is the Lord?

He's THAT good!

The celebration is ALWAYS His.

The following summer, Wes and Andrew, along with their fellow students, graduated and proudly received their diplomas. Wesley called the year's experiences the best of his life and beamed with pride. He had accomplished something he wanted to do and had done it well.

It didn't matter to me if Wes ever cooked another day in his life. What mattered was that my son was able to have a positive schooling experience that proved to him he was capable of doing anything he wanted to do. Wes had matured by years in just one. And the confidence he gained was priceless. The investment was absolutely worth every penny.

The following are the things I learned during Wes's young adult years, as God showed them to me:

Let the Reality Chips Fall

WESLEY'S CHOICE TO try independence without further schooling was not an uncommon one. Many young people have made the same decision and many have been successful in climbing employment ladders while training on the job.

We encouraged Wes to further his education in some official manner, but acknowledged his ability to be successful without doing this. Up to high school graduation, schooling had been a lifetime of struggle for Wesley and held no further interest to him.

By this time, Wes understood how to learn from and change with realities of life. In my opinion, this was an important skill that would serve him well. I knew he would adapt as necessary to meet his own expectations. Our job was simply to support and encourage him to succeed in reaching his goals. The idea was simple. However, deciding when to help or intervene as parents and when not to, was not.

For the young adult who learns to cope best from reality-life lessons, it is important that his/her parents allow as much reality as possible. However, I believe there are also times when parental assistance is appropriate. Deciding which way to respond to a given situation is difficult at best. And the solutions are not perfect. But a solution is a solution because it comes from a decision to solve a problem. Not because it solves EVERY problem or prevents EVERY possible additional problem. No matter the decision, neither is free. Each comes with a price. And during early adult years, the price is usually, literally, MONEY.

Each parent's economic limitations are certainly a deciding factor when considering how much to assist their young adult monetarily. But no matter one's economic status, every parent faces this decision.

When dealing with letting the reality chips fall on my son, God taught me to keep this simple guideline in mind:

SUPPORT TO SUCCEED—Support to Succeed is the practice of rewarding positive behavior and allowing reality/consequences for negative behavior on an adult level. This practice helped me in all matters concerning intervention on behalf of another human being and especially when governing myself as a mother.

For example, if Wesley's poor choices caused him a financial dilemma, then Mom and Dad were unwilling to assist. But if the boy lost his good job because he broke his foot and was unable to drive the company vehicle, a little temporary help from the family was appropriate. During Wes's early twenties, I took things a step further.

When living as a bachelor away from home and partaking in negative behavior, he received no help. His heart wrenching stories accompanying his requests would appear to have no effect on me. But when he decided to clean things up and go to culinary school, Mom was all over it.

God's demonstration of this is recorded repeatedly throughout the Old Testament of the Bible. When dealing with the kings that were given the job of ruling over God's people (a guarded yet granted request to begin with), God dramatically applied the idea of Letting the Reality Chips Fall. The kings and the people were greatly rewarded if they followed the laws God had given them. But if they didn't, the repercussions were undeniable (1 and 2 Samuel; 1 and 2 Kings).

Obviously, we are not God and have not the right to act as God over anyone. No, not even our children. But we ARE faced with decisions concerning them every day. Yet, unlike God, we are not perfect. Therefore, for us, there is no such thing as a decision that makes for a perfect solution. But I found that Support to Succeed could be applied to any situation and was a helpful guideline when dealing with Letting the Reality Chips Fall.

Trust

MANY STRUGGLE WITH trust, and for good reason. Life's experiences have taught them that people can't be trusted. People lie, break promises, fail to follow through with what they say they will do, and go back on their word. Many see their world as full of untrustworthy, manipulating, selfish, and deceitful people. And some experience ultimate disappointment when they feel they cannot even trust themselves.

Oh, how Satan loves this! He relishes in the turmoil he creates and tallies with sinister joy the negative results. Yet, Beelzebub himself trembles in fear with the knowledge that his creation is but a façade and his defeater, the TRUTH, holds reality in His hands (John 16:13; 18:37).

The TRUTH is that most people do not want to lie and do not plan on breaking their promises or going back on their word.

But they do, to their own disappointment. Paul, one of the most influential leaders of the new Christian church, testified to this phenomenon when he wrote, ". . . I want to do what is right, but I don't. Instead, I do the very thing that I hate" (Romans 7:14–25). For many people, the resulting labels of "untrustworthy," "manipulating," "selfish," and "deceitful" (among many others) tag them unmercifully until they believe them to be true and give in to the expected behavior.

The WAY to break this vicious cycle is to show people how Jesus removes the tag, sheds the LIGHT of love on the good that is in them, and shows them the LIFE that is theirs . These simple, yet overwhelmingly powerful traits of God change not only the way we see our fellow man, but mankind itself (John 14:6; Luke 2:25-32).

God trusts that we will act imperfectly, but does not see us as failures. God sees us wrapped in the pure white robe of Jesus.

That's how we look to Him!

When we see the people in our world the way God does, Satan's lie is shattered. We can trust as Jesus did while walking among us. Trust man to be imperfect—forgive him his shortcomings—illuminate his true identity with the light of love—and put full trust in God who works out all things for good. ALL THINGS! (Romans 8:28)

Parents, are you hearing me?

Teach your children a healthy understanding of trust. Teach them to trust in God. But don't just tell them. You must show them. Words will mean nothing until they follow example. Trust your child to be imperfect. Show him/her the way to their own peace with themselves and their fellow man by allowing no labels and illuminating with love the good that they are and the life that is theirs.

Then, BELIEVE in them.

Believe

ONE SURE-FIRE WAY to test our trust in all things is to ask ourselves: "Do I believe?"

And the way to identify our belief is to ask ourselves: "Do I have peace?"

For, if we truly trust God in all things, we must believe that He will make all things good. And if we believe this, we have peace that passes all understanding (Philippians 4:6–7).

If you are a person who struggles with trust and belief, you are not alone. Some personalities are logical and practical and have difficulty believing in something they cannot see. To believe something that cannot be seen is the definition of faith (Hebrews 11:1). Since faith is the basis of Christianity, the idea of Christianity can be difficult for some to wrap their brain around. It seems intangible to the logical mind. But do not despair.

All mankind has been given a heart, a soul that lies deep within that sees and hears God. We just have to learn how to tap into it. To some, it comes as naturally as breathing. To others, it seems impossible. But all have the ability to hear and see with the ears and eyes of their heart (Psalm 119:18; Proverbs 20:12; Ezekiel 3:10; Ephesians 1:17–18). We all know people in our lives that are blessed with this ability. If you are not that person, think about it. You are at least acquainted with, if not know, someone whose faith bubbles from their every pore. Spend some time with this person. Ask them questions. Keep an open mind. Then open a Bible, turn to Matthew 1, and start reading. Spend some more time with your faith friends. Ask more questions. Keep reading. The Lord will take over from there. And you will find peace as you trust and believe.

As your child sees your peace and realizes your confident trust and belief in all things, he/she will immediately understand that it also means you trust and believe in them. And since you trust and believe, you also expect.

Expect

LASTLY, A GOOD way to be certain that we trust and believe is to ask ourselves: "Do I expect? Do I expect the good that I trust and believe in?"

Ah . . . but here is where things can get a little tricky. Once God has worked out trust and belief in our hearts, expecting His good works usually comes easily. Yet, the imperfection of our patience and our limited understanding of time often leave us confused as we try to relate to a God of perfect patience and the Creator of time.

Enter . . . Satan.

Oh, how he loves this one too! He tricks our thinking by using small truths combined with big lies. Satan did this with the first lie he told to the first human he interacted with on earth, and since then, he has perfected his craft (Genesis 3:1–7).

Jesus, having full understanding of the identity of Satan since his fall from heaven, clearly identified him as the liar that he was and is today (John 8:42–44).

Satan reminds us that our friend/family member didn't do what they said they would do (truth). They are untrustworthy (lie). He tells us that people will fail us (truth). People are bad (lie). Satan points out to us that much time has gone by since putting our trust in the Lord over a certain matter and nothing has changed (truth). God cannot be trusted (lie).

We can absolutely expect the good that we trust and believe in to come. But we must remember that the God we trust and believe in is working for our good on His time, not on ours. Therefore, all mankind, though physically living on man's time, is actually in spirit living on God's time. And it is the spirit, our souls, that really matter.

I remember my grandmother and mother praying fervently for many years for my wayward uncle. He had been raised to know God and to understand right and wrong based on God's law. For whatever reason, my uncle became angry with the matter of his religious up-bringing and left the church, appearing to abandon God completely. My mother and grandmother were unable to see their prayers an-swered in complete fruition. But God brought it to pass, and my uncle reunited with his Lord and eventually even returned to the church of his upbringing.

He was on God's time, not on my mother and grandmother's time.

But they both knew their prayers were heard. They trusted, believed, and expected the good that would come even if after their allotted time had passed.

We are all on God's time. And in God's time, we can ABSOLUTELY expect good things.

Here's the bottom line, parents. Big deal!

When we show our children how to trust, believe, and expect God's goodness, they will trust, believe, and expect the good in themselves.

As is common in the life of many postgraduates, Wes struggled to find employment after graduating culinary school. He was able to cook, but not able to get enough hours. Unfortunately, Wes's graduating class emerged from school in the height of a national economic crisis. And after several months, Wesley returned home to attempt to get his feet under him and decide where he might relocate in order to work in his field. But God had other plans . . .

Section III

1

Books of Life

"Close one book . . . open another."

GOD ALWAYS HAS a plan. It bends and turns as we practice our freedom to choose. But for those who love Him, His good plan works with them and brings them to His own.

Like a book, the story of God's plan in motion turns the pages of the years. And the story of His plan takes more than one book. It always has. It always will. But the Lord promises that the good work He starts in us, He will finish. And He will. No matter how many books it takes (Philippians 1:6).

Take Your Pills And Go To Your Room was gradually written over a ten-year period. Each day that I sat down to write and share what had happened and what God had taught me over the months or years that had passed, I was blessed and humbled with every word that filled the pages. Much of the time what I intended to write did not make it to the page and what did was a revelation at that very moment, a realization in real time.

Praise God!

The Lord never allowed me to write when angry, frustrated, or fatigued. And even when writing and reliving these moments, He enlightened and encouraged me.

As my fingers flew across the keyboard, my heart took flight as well.

For there is no better way to realize what God has done then to relive the past in the knowledge of the future. The experience has allowed me to see how God works in His time and to trust that He will do it again.

"And what of Wesley?" you ask.

Ah . . . read about that in the next book.

At the time of this book's closing, many changes had taken place in my own life.

Kevin and I had divorced.

The pastor of my church and I had a disagreement concerning my divorce, and I left the church of my upbringing.

I became fatigued at work and retired from the job that I loved after twenty years in the business.

My brothers continued to struggle with alcoholism.

Jami's best friend, Katie, who grew up spending a lot of time with us, lost her grandmother in the height of her mother's destructive alcoholism and faced threatening custody issues.

Sharing these changes of my life after writing a book full of the Lord's success with my children may seem anticlimactic or even antisuccessful.

But the actual experience of it was not. It was my true story. It was real.

And, reality is, that at the end of every story, something good has always happened.

For, there is HOPE and BEAUTY in every day. There is PROGRESS and VICTORY in every hour. And there is an abundance of LAUGHTER and LOVE in every moment.

Divorce is not the end of something but the beginning of something else.

God does not see any of us as members of particular churches, but as beloved members of His family.

Paramedics have a lifespan, and praise God it's shorter than mine.

To struggle is to be made stronger. Getting stronger is recovery.

And it is of the greatest honor and blessing to be CHOSEN by a child.

We read in the Bible that after the death of their father, Jacob,

Joseph's brothers feared that he would then retaliate for the evil they had committed against him. But Joseph believed and had seen God's hand in it all. He comforted his brothers by explaining that God used the evil they had done for good (Genesis 50:15–21).

Satan may work evil against us, but God uses it for good, ALWAYS.

As I write these words of the last chapter, the revelation of timing and symbolism settles over me like a comforting blanket. The book of God's plan in motion for one part of my life must close in order that the next book may begin. I look forward with excitement to whatever He has in store for me and to writing it down.

Yet, how does anyone close a book about all that God has taught them through the experience of raising a child with ADHD? (The cursor on the computer screen sits flashing.) It's overwhelming, and rightly so. Documenting EVERY experience is impossible. So much is missing. But even as I write these words, the Lord comforts me with the realization that even the books of the Bible share only highlights. And yet, it is perfectly enough. God makes all that is His perfectly enough.

I am perfectly enough.

You are perfectly enough.

The children are perfectly enough.

The child/children that you read this book for were purposely placed in your life because you are perfectly enough.

Do you know what this means, my friends?

It means that we can do ANYTHING!

We can do ALL THINGS through our Lord Jesus Christ, who strengthens and enlightens us! Anything is possible for us as children of God. Therefore, anything is possible for YOUR child/children of God (Philippians 4:13).

Your book has already begun. It is a crazy—wild—energetic—and beautiful story—full of life! It is funny! (Think about it. It really is.) It is your story of God's plan in motion. Write it down!

Life is an adventure. Give it all that you have. What you have is what God gives to you.

God has richly blessed you.